Montana's

MISSOURI & MUSSELSHELL RIVERS

And Their Tributaries

TEXT AND PHOTOS BY RICK AND SUSIE GRAETZ
AERIAL PHOTOGRAPHY BY LARRY MAYER

The Montana Series

10

NUMBER TEN

PHOTOGRAPHY CONTRIBUTIONS BY:

Chuck Haney and John Lambing

Tall and dark, LaBarge Rock has been a landmark from steamboaters to present-day canoeists.
RICK AND SUSIE GRAETZ

Rick and Susie Graetz
P.O. Box 1707, Helena, Montana 59624
thisismontana@aol.com

Book design by GingerBee Creative, Helena, Montana

All color and prepress work done in Montana, U.S.A.
Printed in Hong Kong
Softcover: ISBN 1-891152-46-7
Hardcover: ISBN 1-891152-47-5

Front Cover: Missouri River below Culbertson on the Missouri River Ranch. RICK AND SUSIE GRAETZ
Back Cover: Confluence of the Missouri and Musselshell rivers at the UL Bend. LARRY MAYER

NOTES ON THE MISSOURI AND MUSSELSHELL

"... by every rule of nomenclature, the Missouri being the main stream and the upper Mississippi the tributary, the name of the former should have been given precedence, and the great-river should have been called Missouri from the Rocky Mountains to the Gulf of Mexico." Many people, especially Montanans, agree with this unknown author's statement. However, the Mississippi was explored first and therefore designated the primary stem, thus leaving the Missouri to receive tributary status. Also included in the argument is whether or not the Yellowstone River, the Missouri's other major partner, should have received top billing ... another question for the ages.

Whatever the Missouri's national standing, for Montana it was a lifeline ... a moving highway that gave birth to our state. On the way to the nation's heartland, it collects all of our memories and first written history. It is our great river. One nameless writer, speaking of the attributes of other Montana rivers, said it well. *"The Missouri is all these and more ... It is the Milk and Musselshell, the Wind and the Sun, the Big Hole and the Beaverhead and the Marias, streams of mountains and of plains moving toward their compulsive rendezvous with the distant ocean, carving shadows upon rocks, giving perspective to great spaces almost anesthetic in their dizzying emptiness, reflecting blazing suns and mellow moons, bordering their shores with tender trees of willows sweet to the eyes of men in a nearly treeless land."*

When the Missouri contacts the Mississippi, 2,546 miles of flow will have been attained, making it longer than the entire Mississippi and more than three times the length of the Yellowstone.

While the Yellowstone River's original water sources collect very quickly — within a couple of miles — before sending the Yellowstone on its way, major contributors to the Missouri's beginnings initially cover a great deal of ground and establish significant identifications of their own prior to joining in. Consider the Jefferson with its upstream continuations the Beaverhead and Red Rock rivers, together they take in 294 miles. And when the Jefferson, Madison and Gallatin come together to develop the mother river, each arrives swiftly carrying large quantities of water.

From the melding of its tributaries, this celebrated entity will cover 734 beautiful Montana river miles before picking up the Yellowstone just across the Montana/North Dakota line.

Then there's the Musselshell! Tumbling, twisting and turning from its mountain origins, it spreads out on the high prairie of central Montana collecting history, while passing through some of the state's most pleasing scenic beauty. Island mountain ranges greet its passage as it eases towards the Missouri at the UL Bend.

The great Indian nations who followed the migration of the bison valued both rivers. In their winter camp of 1804–1805 near present day Bismarck, N.D., the Corps of Discovery learned from the Hidatsa Tribe of the uncharted country they would pass through as they moved against the Missouri's current. The Hidatsa, who traveled to the Rockies to hunt, told Lewis and Clark of the *"shell river"* and its headwaters.

We present the story of these two physically and historically linked Montana rivers.

RICK AND SUSIE GRAETZ
August 17, 2004
Prickly Pear Valley, Montana

▲ The Missouri near Culbertson. CHUCK HANEY

MONTANA'S MISSOURI RIVER

August 12, 1805, Meriwether Lewis penned in his journals, *"the road was still plain, I therefore did not dispare of shortly finding a passage over the mountains and of tasting the waters of the great Columbia this evening. At the distance of four miles further the road took us to the most distant fountain of the waters of the mighty Missouri in search of which we have spent so many toilsome days in wristless nights."* Lewis was describing today's Distant Fountain Spring, part of Trail Creek, flowing off the east side of the Continental Divide at Lemhi Pass. Climbing above the trickle, Lewis became the first known white man to have stepped onto and across Montana's Continental Divide.

However, in terms of the most distant waters, he was a bit off. That honor is reserved for a spring and Hellroaring Creek coming off the Montana side of the Continental Divide just below 9,846-foot Mt. Jefferson at the extreme eastern end of the Centennial Range. Hellroaring has a short life; it is hastily consumed by Red Rock Creek, which begins off the Divide below Red Rock Mountain at Lillian Lake 9,000 feet above sea level.

Standing at the headwaters of the Missouri at Three Forks on July 28, 1805, Lewis noted, *"Both Capt. C. and myself corrisponded in opinion, with rispect, to the impropriety of calling either of these streams the Missouri and accordingly agreed to name them. we called the S.W. Fork, that which we meant to ascend, Jefferson's river in honor of Thomas Jefferson. the Middle fork we called Madison's River in honor of James Madison, and the S.E. Fork Gallitian's river in honor of Albert Gallitian."*

▲ The Centennial Range — the origin of the farthest trickle of the Missouri River.

RICK AND SUSIE GRAETZ

◀ Red Rock Lakes in the Centennial Valley.

RICK AND SUSIE GRAETZ

▲ Beaverhead Rock and the Beaverhead River north of Dillon.
RICK AND SUSIE GRAETZ

▸ The Jefferson River in the Tobacco Root Mountains.
CHUCK HANEY

At this point, the three tributaries make their presence well known. The Madison and Jefferson, each close to 100 feet wide, join and then cover a short distance before meeting the equally broad Gallatin. Of all three tributaries, the Jefferson, counting its suppliers, drains the largest area and the Gallatin the smallest.

THE JEFFERSON RIVER

The Jefferson, Madison and Gallatin rivers are famous for forming the mighty Missouri River. But of the three, it is the Jefferson River and its many upper components that hold a lofty ranking in history. It was this southwest Montana river that the Corps of Discovery used after they left the origin of the Missouri to take them to their land route across the massive Rocky Mountains.

In their journals, Lewis and Clark named the entire length of the now Jefferson and Beaverhead rivers *"Jefferson's River,"* but today's Jefferson begins where the Big Hole (*"Wisdom"* to the Expedition) and Beaverhead rivers mix their waters north of Twin Bridges and downstream from the entrance of the Ruby (*"Philanthropy"*) River. The Beaverhead originates farther south at the joining of Red Rock River and Horse Prairie Creek — the actual confluence is now under the waters of Clark Canyon Reservoir. The Jefferson River is complicated with numerous tributaries responsible for its creation.

Red Rock River falls out of the mountains and courses through a most beautiful setting, the Centennial Valley and the Red Rock Lakes National Wildlife Refuge. Slowing to fill Upper and Lower Red Rock lakes, it offers haven and nesting ground for species such as the endangered trumpeter swan. Marshes, meadows, creeks, sand hills and two lakes make up the almost 45,000-acre refuge, of which 32,350 acres are designated wilderness.

If it weren't for the wildlife refuge, few travelers would make their way through this nearly 40-mile-long valley. From the slowly disappearing town of Monida, just off of Interstate 15 and Monida Pass, a dirt and gravel road winds its way east through windswept hills of sage before easing down into the Centennial Valley. Peaks of the 10,000-foot Centennial Mountains and the Continental Divide rise abruptly on the valley's southern flank. The 9,000- and 10,000-foot summits of the Gravelly and Snowcrest ranges guard the drainage's north side.

The country and most of the activities of this 6,600-foot-high broad and flat basin haven't changed much in the last one hundred years. Cattlemen first ventured into the place in 1876, establishing what are now some of the oldest ranches in the state.

In the 1880s, determined Yellowstone National Park tourists coming from Salt Lake City, Utah, traveled by train to Monida and then endured a two-day stagecoach trip through the valley to the Park. It was necessary to overnight at Lakeview, now the headquarters for the Refuge and home to several folks.

During the homestead era of the early 1900s, Lakeview and the surrounding area permanently hosted nearly 400 people. The stores, saloons and a hotel were prosperous until the drought years and Great Depression coupled with the struggle against tough winters ended the hopes of most of the population. Many of the homesteads were bought out as land was acquired for the wildlife reserve.

At the western end of the Centennial Valley, Red Rock River enters the 13-mile-long Lima

▲ Near Silver Star – the valley of the Jefferson River and the Tobacco Root Mountains.
RICK AND SUSIE GRAET

▶ The Madison River near the three forks in the Gallatin Valley.
RICK AND SUSIE GRAETZ

Reservoir. Until this point, the river has been extending westward; now, beyond the man-made lake, it begins a northwesterly setting until it meets Clark Canyon Reservoir and the waters of Horse Prairie Creek entering from the west. Here, Interstate 15 guides fast-moving traffic between Montana and Idaho, with most of the travelers oblivious to the historic topography they are passing through.

Horse Prairie Creek takes its initial waters from the Continental Divide below Deadman's Pass southwest of Clark Canyon Reservoir. Out in the sagebrush flats of this remote ranching country, it picks up Trail Creek coming off the Divide near Lemhi Pass. Frying Pan Creek, Bear Creek and Spring Creek also contribute their waters to Horse Prairie. After meeting, they flow eastward toward Clark Canyon passing the settlement of Grant and its old hotel and stagecoach stop. A post office was established here in 1899, but was discontinued in the late 1950s.

All this water pools together in Clark Canyon Reservoir, then after squeezing through a gap, it emerges as the Beaverhead River and heads toward Dillon and one of the largest of the intermountain valleys of southwest Montana — home to many multi-generational family ranches. Several creeks, including historic Grasshopper Creek on the west, as well as Blacktail Deer Creek on the east, add to the Beaverhead. Grasshopper Creek, "*Willard Creek*" to Lewis and Clark, was the site in July, 1862, of Montana's first major gold strike and led to the founding of Bannack, Montana's initial territorial capital.

Dillon, the "*capital*" of far southwest Montana, originated because the laying of railroad tracks came to a temporary stop here. In 1880, Sydney Dillon, president of the Utah and Northern Railroad (later the Union Pacific), was building rail from Utah to Butte when he was blocked just 60 miles south of his goal by a rancher who refused to sell the right-of-way across his property.

The railroad construction crew population spent the winter of 1880–1881 in a makeshift town of tents and rickety wood buildings in the Beaverhead Valley. The lengthy delay allowed for the establishment of businesses to serve the laborers. By summer, Sydney Dillon received his right-of-way and the railroad continued northward. But a town, named for the entrepreneur, remained.

For a while, the Beaverhead Valley and Dillon were the state's largest wool shipping area and also profited from nearby gold, silver and lead mines. Presently, this community of about 3,800 people is known for its historic architecture. Landmarks such as the 1888 Dillon Tribune Building and the Metlen Hotel, finished in 1897, stand out and add to the feel of the Old West town that Dillon is.

The University of Montana Western serves as an anchor for Dillon, the seat of Beaverhead County — a province larger in size than the combined states of Connecticut and Rhode Island.

Along the river north of town is a large limestone formation resembling a swimming beaver known as Beaverhead Rock. In the summer of 1805, Lewis and Clark knew they would soon have to cross the Rocky Mountains in order to reach the Columbia River and ultimately the Pacific Ocean. As signs of an early autumn began to appear, there came also a sense of urgency to find the Shoshone Indians and acquire horses from them.

On the evening of August 8, Lewis penned "*the Indian woman* (Sacajawea) *recognized the … hill she says her nation calls the beavers head from a conceived resemblance of its figure to the head of that animal. She assures us that we shall either find her people on this river or on the river immediately west of its source.*" Spirits and the journey's outlook took a rise!

In the area of this landmark and in many other places, the Beaverhead River is a slow, meandering waterway with numerous channels and banks choked with brushy vegetation. Lewis often mentioned these conditions in his journal entries.

As the Beaverhead River progresses in a northeasterly direction, it brings on board the 103-mile-long Ruby River flowing in from the southeast. Just beyond the meeting of these two rivers north of the town of Twin Bridges, the Big Hole River, a 155-mile-long blue ribbon fishing stream, joins the Beaverhead and together they begin the Jefferson River's momentum. The name Twin Bridges comes from a toll bridge built by the Lott Brothers in 1867 that stretched across the Big Hole and the Beaverhead Rivers.

By 1884, Twin Bridges was a hub of commerce for southwest Montana and three stagecoaches a day stopped there. The State Orphan Home was the largest employer until it was closed in 1975. Now the town's claim to fame is the world-class trout fishing found in the area.

Beyond Twin Bridges, the valley narrows and the now Jefferson River runs through a bottomland defined by the Tobacco Root Mountains to the east and the Highland Mountains on the west. It passes the little burg of Silver Star, so named because it was a supply point for the silver miners and the only speck of civilization between Virginia City and Helena. The Silver Star post office was established in 1869, making the town one of the oldest in the state.

In some notes from the expedition while traversing the Tobacco Root Valley on August 2, 1805, Lewis described, "*the tops of these mountains were yet partially covered with snow while we in the valley were suffocated nearly with the intense heat of the midday sun. the nights are so could that two blankets are not more than sufficient covering.*" This day they christened the present Whitetail Creek by the town of Whitehall "*Birth Creek*" in honor of Clark's 35th birthday the day before. Lewis camped that night in the heart of the valley at Waterloo, just above the one-time raucous mining camp of Silver Star.

As the Jefferson reaches the northern tip of the Tobacco Root Mountains, it swings east and prepares for its final run. The next community it touches is Cardwell, named for Edward Cardwell and known as the birthplace of former NBC News anchor Chet Huntley. Mining in the nearby mountains at one time kept it going, but there is not much left now.

From Cardwell, the river pinches into a tight canyon. High above the streambed on the north side of the mountain is the Lewis and Clark Caverns State Park. Neither Lewis nor Clark ever saw the caverns, but Clark came close to them while searching for the Shoshone.

Past the caverns, and approximately 24 miles from its end, the river enters the wide Gallatin Valley. On the way, Willow Creek ("*Philosophy River*" to the Corps), enters the Jefferson. Finally, just east of Three Forks, running nearly 100-feet wide, the Jefferson, its job nearly completed, plows into the Madison River. Together, the two rivers cover about one mile before meeting the equally broad Gallatin River.

▲ The Parker Homestead State Park just off the Jefferson River.
RICK AND SUSIE GRAETZ

◀ Fishing the Madison River below Hebgen Lake.
RICK AND SUSIE GRAETZ

▲ Quake Lake formed by the Madison Canyon earthquake.
RICK AND SUSIE GRAETZ

▶ The Madison River.
RICK AND SUSIE GRAETZ

The Madison River

On September 19, 1870, after exploring the future Yellowstone National Park for more than a month, the Washburn Expedition camped in the shadow of 7,560-foot National Park Mountain. Here on the grassy meadows surrounding the Madison River's inception at the confluence of the Firehole and Gibbon rivers, they discussed the need to protect this magical and wondrous place.

After returning to Montana Territory, the participants of the Washburn party wrote newspaper and magazine articles and gave speeches in support of their findings. This prompted the U.S. government to sponsor the Hayden Surveys. These surveys led to President Ulysses Grant's signing an act creating Yellowstone National Park, the nation's and the world's first national park, on March 1, 1872.

The Firehole River begins its journey on the Madison Plateau and Continental Divide just south of Old Faithful near Shoshone Lake. From there it heads north, gathering steam and speed as it maneuvers through three geyser basins.

As the Gibbon River leaves its birthplace in the Grebe Lake area northwest of the Grand Canyon of the Yellowstone, it takes a wild ride through two geyser basins, several rapids, and a dramatic 84-foot plunge over Gibbon Falls before rendezvousing with the Firehole to form the Madison River.

Named for President Jefferson's Secretary of State, James Madison, the newly-made river commences its 150-mile run by passing herds of bison and elk as it meanders west to northwest before crossing out of the Park and resting briefly in Hebgen and Quake lakes, site of the Madison River Canyon Earthquake.

On August 17, 1959, at about 11:37 p.m., the ground in the area of Hebgen Lake began to pitch and tremble; a major 7.5 earthquake was underway. Man-made structures moved, split apart and some collapsed. For almost 12 hours, the usually placid water in Hebgen Lake sloshed back and forth like a tidal wave. The first few breakers, estimated to be 20 feet high, were large enough to flow over the dam.

A few miles downstream in the Madison Canyon, part of the mountainside, shattered by the tremor, began to fall away. The avalanche, with a terrible roaring and grinding, crushed and buried campers, cars and trailers. Folks tell of being knocked down by a violent air blast and then being engulfed by a huge wave of water displaced from the Madison River.

As repeated aftershocks shook the area, boulders and rock falls continued to assault the survivors throughout the night. It wasn't until daylight that the immensity of the landslide became apparent. A nearly mile-long section of the north-facing flank of a mountain crest, about 1,300 feet above the river floor, had broken loose and moved across the canyon as a sheet. The momentum of the slide was such that its front rode about 400 feet up the opposite canyon wall. Twenty-eight people were killed, 19 of them entombed beneath the rubble.

Since Madison Valley was blocked by the landslide, the waves that crested Hebgen Dam and water which is normally released through the spillway began to build up on the east side of the rock and rubble wall and Quake Lake began to form. By August 31, it was five miles long, 150 feet deep, and rising by nine feet daily. On September 9, only 22 days after the quake and just as the waters were reaching the top of the dam, a mile-long spillway was finished and a ruinous flood averted.

The deadly consequences of the earthquake stole the Madison River's innocence and left a vivid reminder of the devastation nature's power can render.

Once the Madison River bids farewell to the earthquake-scarred mountainside and leaves the stillness of Quake Lake behind, it rushes, full of life, out into the spacious Madison Valley where it holds court as one of Montana's premiere fly-fishing destinations. From the outlet of the lake to the Hwy 87 bridge on the road to Raynolds Pass and Idaho's Henry Lake, the river is best described as bad floating water, with huge drops, big boulders and a wild run. The best drifting for on-the-water fishing and just plain *"running the river"* begins at the bridge and ends 48 miles away at Ennis. In between, the river is shallow and fast; some have called it one continuous riffle.

Flowing in a northerly direction flanked by the Madison and Gravelly mountain ranges, the Madison touches Ennis, the river's *"fly fishing capital."* A tidy little town with the look of the Old West, it was named after William Ennis, one of the Madison Valley's first settlers. He built a store in the vicinity of the present town site in 1879 and then when the post office opened in 1881, he became the first postmaster. For 86 years thereafter, a member of the Ennis family managed the local post office.

Five miles below Ennis, the Madison slows and spreads out into Ennis Lake. Acting as an enormous solar heat collector, the lake's water is warmed, creating a treat for the folks who recreate below the dam. However, the temperate water wreaks havoc with the previously excellent trout populace.

Whitewater fans revel in the difficult 10-mile wilderness stretch of Bear Trap Canyon with its legendary Double Drop, White Horse, Kitchen Sink and Greenwave rapids. This beautiful part of the river cuts through the western edge of the Lee Metcalf Wilderness. On any summer day, a colorful armada of inner-tubers, rafters and fishermen populates the more sedate 11 miles from the Warm Springs to the Greycliff river access sites.

It is at this point the Madison breaks away from the road. Now forging the last leg of the journey to the Gallatin Valley, it passes through an isolated section featuring 100-foot-high gray colored bluffs.

Several miles northeast of the town of Three Forks, the nearly 100-foot-wide Madison converges with the Jefferson. The U.S. Geologic Survey claims the Missouri starts at this point, but history and common acceptance dictate that the Missouri doesn't start until the two combined rivers cover a short distance and meet the Gallatin River. At that point, the Missouri River comes to life.

GALLATIN RIVER

In July 1805, Captains Meriwether Lewis and William Clark gave the Secretary of the Treasury's name to what they considered to be the southeast fork of the Missouri. As a member of President Thomas Jefferson's cabinet, Albert Gallatin, as one biographer wrote, *"played a vital part in establishing the financial soundness of a new nation."* Other than the famous namesake and the historic spot where it expires, the Gallatin River — the smallest of the Missouri's tributaries — carries little history of note. However, what it lacks in historical significance, it more than makes up for in topographic beauty. The upper Gallatin River Canyon is one of Montana's most scenic valleys.

▲ The Gallatin River Meadows in Yellowstone National Park.
RICK AND SUSIE GRAETZ

◄ The Gallatin River in the Gallatin Canyon.
RICK AND SUSIE GRAETZ

The Gallatin River as it winds through the Gallatin Canyon.
RICK AND SUSIE GRAETZ

U.S. Hwy 191, the ribbon of road passing through today's Gallatin Canyon, was once a rough Indian and wildlife thoroughfare following steep grades with several fords of the Gallatin River. In 1883, Gallatin County commissioners hired a survey group to determine whether a road from Salesville, now Gallatin Gateway, to Yellowstone National Park would be feasible. The finding was in the affirmative and the Gallatin Valley had its first taste of tourism when the road was completed.

In the northwest corner of Yellowstone National Park, Three Rivers Peak and Gallatin Lake send off the Gallatin River. Initially, it tumbles through prime grizzly bear habitat and a narrow, avalanche-prone valley before easing into the wide, grass-covered Gallatin River Meadows. There it performs sweeping meanders surrounded by gently rising mountains of mostly burned timber, the result of forest fires in 1979 and 1988. At this point, the river is in the Wyoming portion of the Park and must log 15 miles before reaching the boundary.

Not long after leaving Yellowstone National Park, the Gallatin wedges itself into the constricted and spectacular Gallatin River Canyon. Formed by steep rises of the Gallatin Range looking down from the east and the Madison Range across the way, this stretch, up to the canyon's abrupt demise southwest of Bozeman, is a fishing, kayaking, floating and photographic paradise.

From the entrance of the West Fork of the Gallatin at the resort town of Big Sky to Squaw Creek, a distance of 17 miles, one will find some of Montana's most popular white water, which includes technical rapids, boulders and especially in high water, enormous waves. House Rock, visible from the road, is a favorite spot for spectators to watch the action, particularly during spring run off.

While in the canyon, the Gallatin picks up new water from the Taylor Fork, West Fork, and Spanish Creek, among others.

The quick ending of the canyon walls allows the river to spill and spread into the ample and fertile Gallatin Valley, a once beautiful pastoral land now sprouting unsightly subdivisions.

Twelve miles before its end, and two miles north of Manhattan, the Gallatin meets the East Gallatin River, its largest tributary. The East Gallatin is formed when Bridger Creek, arriving from the north, and Bozeman Creek, from the south, converge.

One hundred and fifteen miles from its initiation, the Gallatin, now a forceful river, joins the already combined Madison and Jefferson rivers to create the Big Missouri.

Three Forks and Headwaters State Park

A labyrinth of channels, willow bottoms, islands and a general mix of wetlands interact to piece together the headwaters of the Missouri River.

From here, the point where the three forks — the Jefferson, Gallatin and Madison rivers — join as one, the great Missouri River begins an odyssey. Having had the starring role in the creation of a state and as a route of western expansion, the Missouri River had few equals. Missouri Headwaters State Park, at the three forks, gathers in and documents well the river's illustrious past in the chronology of our Montana heritage through interpretive signs and displays.

History was vivid at the union of the three rivers. Long before whites trespassed, the place was a natural crossroad, camping spot, hunting area, meeting and battleground for the Natives, including the Hidatsa, Blackfeet, Shoshone, Crow, Nez Perce, Kootenai and Salish. Today, faint pictographs, the only physical evidence of the passing of indigenous cultures at the forks, are found in a small cave.

Captains Meriwether Lewis and William Clark and their fellow explorers were the first documented white travelers to witness the area. By the time they reached the headwaters, the Corps of Discovery had already spent three months in what would become Montana. Weatherwise, time was running short; anxious to trade for horses to enable them to cross the mountains, they had hoped to have encountered the Shoshone Indians by now.

July 25, 1805, Captain Clark, in spite of feet painfully blistered and ravaged with prickly pear thorns, was traveling overland and a couple of days ahead of Lewis when he arrived at the joining of the three rivers. Quickly choosing to explore the "*North fork*" (soon to be named Jefferson's River), which in his estimation was the route to the Columbia, he left a note for Lewis and spent the next two days in search of the Shoshone. He contracted "*a high fever & akeing in all my bones,*" but found no sign of the Indians. Reluctantly he turned back, crossed over to the middle fork — to be named the Madison — and camped for the night explaining, "*I continue to be verry unwell fever verry high.*"

Clark spent the nights of July 25 and 26 at two separate camps on "*Philosophy River*" (Willow Creek) near the present village of Willow Creek, just a few miles southwest of the Three Forks town site.

On the morning of July 27, Lewis and his men met up with Clark at the three forks. Lewis' journal entry for that night read: "*the country opens suddonly to extensive and beatifull plains and meadows which appeared to be surrounded in every direction with distant and lofty mountains; supposing this*

▲ An old cabin on the Gallatin River near its confluence with Spanish Creek.
RICK AND SUSIE GRAETZ

▶ The Crimson Bluffs along the Missouri near Townsend.
RICK AND SUSIE GRAETZ

to be the Three Forks of the Missouri I halted the party." Lewis then walked about a half mile up the Gallatin and *"ascended the point of a high limestone clift* (Lewis's Rock) *from whence I commanded a most perfect view of the neighbouring country."* The explorer was beholding the Spanish Peaks and Madison Range to the south, the Gallatin Range to the southeast and the Tobacco Root Mountains in his southwest view field. He could also see the Bridger Range directly to the east. In between was the lush, wide valley of the Gallatin River.

Good news came as Sacajawea recognized the area and informed them that this was the exact place her people were encamped when the Hidatsa had captured her five years earlier.

When the Corps returned to St. Louis in September of 1806, fur trappers were already on their way to the new country. In North Dakota, after meeting a group of trappers heading upriver, John Colter of the Expedition left Lewis and Clark and return to the country he fondly recalled. In 1808, Colter and John Potts were trapping at the three forks when they encountered Blackfeet hunters and warriors. Potts was killed and Colter was given a chance to escape. The Blackfeet took his clothes and allowed him to run for his life. Grabbing a spear from his closest pursuer, Colter was able to make the kill and create a diversion. Upon reaching the Madison River, he hid among the driftwood. The Indians gave up the search and Colter began a seven-day *"walk,"* minus clothes or footwear, to a trading post 200 miles away at the confluence of the Bighorn and Yellowstone rivers east of modern-day Billings,.

Despite this incident, Colter returned several times to the forks. In 1810, he was part of a group that established a trading post here. When Indians attacked the post and killed several traders, Colter left and vowed never to return.

In 1862, Frank Dunbar built the first home in the Gallatin Valley at the headwaters. By 1863, settlers were arriving and Gallatin City came alive on the land between the point where the Jefferson and Madison are already joined and the Gallatin enters. The goal was to make this a river *"port,"* but the founders didn't consider, or know about, the five *"great falls"* well to the north that blocked steamboat traffic. When the pioneers realized their town had no future, they abandoned it. Then in 1865, Gallatin City II was established. A ferry crossing accessed the mining camps to the west. The town served as an agricultural center until 1883 when the railroad, coming through the Gallatin Valley, passed it two miles to the south. Even before that, Bozeman's growing presence spelled the end to Gallatin City's second try. For a while, it was the seat of Gallatin County and boasted a flour mill, stores, a stage stop and a hotel. All that remains now is the skeleton of the hotel.

During Gallatin City's final years, Three Forks' predecessor, called *"An English Nobility Colony"* in the book Names on the Face of Montana, sputtered along with a toll bridge that spanned the area's wetlands and the Madison and Jefferson rivers. It wasn't until 1908, when the Milwaukee RR arrived, that the current town of Three Forks gained a hold in its present and much dryer location and grew with the railroad.

The landscape at the headwaters has much the same appearance as when the Corps of Discovery and the fur trappers spent time here. One of Montana's historical staging areas, those periods still permeate the atmosphere of this place. And there is nothing shy about it. The Gallatin, Madison and Jefferson come in with plenty of water and power to give the Missouri an enviable starting surge — no trickles, springs or snowmelt to kick it off. At the exact place where the big Missouri goes forth, there is no mistaking it for a stream. It is clearly a major river from the get go.

Today's Missouri Headwaters State Park, which takes in the area surrounding the forks, was the idea of Clark Maudlin. While visiting the place with his family in 1928, he recognized its historical importance and set out to purchase the land and then donated it to the state of Montana. The park opened in 1951.

Leaving the Three Forks

Upon departing the three forks, the newly formed Missouri is almost immediately neatly tucked into a mini-gorge and then, only 16 miles from its inception, the Toston Reservoir and Dam decelerate its flow. After traversing the *"Little Gates of the Mountains,"* so noted on Clark's map of July 25, 1805, as *"2d range of mts — little gate,"* near the small village of Toston, the river will soon ply the last of the big southwest valleys. Officially established when the post office opened in 1882, and named after a local rancher, Tosten bills itself as *"the first town on the Missouri."*

Wandering north between the Bridger and Belt mountains on its east flank and the Elkhorn Mountains to the west, the river threads its way first through Broadwater Valley and then finds the Prickly Pear Valley and Helena area.

Early on the morning of July 24, 1805, Lewis and his men *"passed a remarkable bluff of a crimson coloured earth on Stard. intermixed with Stratas of black and brick red slate."* These are now called the Crimson Bluffs, located about a mile southwest of Townsend.

Like many Montana communities tied to the coming of the rails, Townsend's title comes from a connection to the railroads. In this case it was named for Mrs. Charles Wright, whose husband was president of the Great Northern at one time. Her maiden name was Townsend. At first, the community was called Centerville, but the name changed when the steel road reached the area in 1883. The newspaper in Helena said it would soon become one of the most important towns in Montana and called it the "Metropolis of the Missouri Valley." Townsend, the seat of Broadwater County, has always owed its prosperity to the surrounding ranches and farms. Recreation on the Missouri and Canyon Ferry Lake now adds to the town's well being.

Construction of Canyon Ferry Dam began in May, 1948, and was completed in June, 1954. Named for the ferry that traversed the river before the dam and bridge were built, the resulting lake has 76 miles of shoreline.

By this time, the Missouri River has covered 42 miles of gentle meanders. Now it prepares to enter an almost 70-mile-long stretch, including 26 miles in Canyon Ferry Reservoir, of a series of Canyon Ferry, Hauser and Holter lakes and dams. All three dams were built to harness the Missouri and create electric power; recreational use was secondary.

Between Townsend and Helena, the river is covering country that gold settled. Just north of Townsend, up in the Big Belt Mountains on the east side of Canyon Ferry Lake, was an extraordinarily rich placer gold find. In December of 1864, two Confederate soldiers struck it big here. They named this site Confederate Gulch after their political leanings and built four cabins to settle into for the winter. The path in the snow among the cabins formed a perfect diamond, so they christened

Sunrise over the frozen Missouri near Townsend.
JOHN LAMBING

Looking North on Canyon Ferry Lake.
LARRY MAYER

▲ The Big Belt Mountains and Canyon Ferry Lake north of Townsend.
RICK AND SUSIE GRAETZ

▶ The Missouri River near Wolf Creek.
RICK AND SUSIE GRAETZ

the camp Diamond City. At one time 5,000 people crowded into the narrow canyon. It was said that some of the hillside prospectors garnered more than $1,000 worth of gold from a single pan of gravel. The big boom was over by 1870, and in 1880 only a couple of people remained.

On the afternoon of July 14, 1864, four men, nursing their bad luck in the gulches and camps of Alder Gulch and Grasshopper Creek to the southwest, and who had been following rumors of gold to the north in the Kootenai country, returned to a gulch they had prospected a bit earlier. This was to be their *"last chance."* Digging to bedrock in a canyon below today's Mount Ascension and Mount Helena, they hit pay dirt. A camp called Last Chance — later Helena — was mapped out and, as other would-be-miners and prospectors migrated to the Prickly Pear Valley, became an overnight boom.

In August, 1865, the post office was established, and 10 years later in 1875, Helena became the third Territorial capital, taking over from Virginia City. On November 8, 1889, when Montana became a state, Helena was named the capital, although that status wasn't permanent until 1894 when Helena won out over Anaconda in an election.

The search for gold continued in the myriad surrounding gulches and canyons, including those in the Big Belt Mountains. More ore was found and additional camps, most of which have long since disappeared, were established.

In the gravels of the Eldorado Bar, a former gold placer claim just off of the Missouri, modern-day prospectors search for sapphires.

Downstream from Canyon Ferry Lake, and northwest of Helena, the Missouri's waters edge the western perimeter of the Gates of the Mountains Wilderness. Here, the river's channel narrows to knife its way through steep limestone walls. Lewis's journal notes of July 19, 1805, read in part: "... *this evening we entered much the most remarkable clifts that we have yet seen. these clifts rise from the waters edge on either side perpendicularly to the hight of about 1200 feet ... the towering and projecting rocks in many places seem ready to tumble on us ... for the distance of 5 ¾ miles ... the river appears to have woarn a passage just the width of it's channel or 150 yds. it is deep from side to side nor is ther in the 1st 3 miles of this distance a spot ... on which a man could rest the soal of his foot ... from the singular appearance of this place I called it the gates of the rocky mountains."*

As the river passes through the Gates, it takes on the Adels, an extension of the Big Belt Mountains. Here, held back by the last of the upriver dams, the Missouri fills Holter Lake. After the dam, it sweeps by the east side of a recreation community, named for Warren Craig who built the first cabin here in 1886. It is now relatively free to run unobstructed for 89 miles until meeting the Sun River at Great Falls.

Beyond the Adels, the Missouri bids farewell to the Northern Rocky Mountains. Near the community of Cascade, a sleepy farm and ranch town with one foot on the prairie and the other in the mountains, the mighty river makes a transition from wide valleys and generous peaks to the open plain where it will hit full stride with space to spread and grow.

In 1886, the Central Montana Railroad, later the Great Northern, established a rail crew camp here in the process of laying down tracks on the west side of the Missouri River. It took root as the town of Dodge. In 1887, when the railroad was completed, Cascade became the new name. Some accounts claim the name is for the great falls of the Missouri, 30 miles to the north. It is more likely that Cascade was named after waterfalls on the Missouri upriver. In 1914, at the height of the homestead boom, more than 50 businesses were thriving in Cascade. Depression, drought, and the growth of Great Falls eventually took people away and the town quieted down to the approximate 700 people who live there today.

The Missouri Meets the Prairie

As the river puts Cascade behind, it looks out toward the west and the distant Rocky Mountain Front, the range of mountains that gave Montana its label, *"Land of the Shining Mountains."* It also observes to its west an isolated landform, Charlie Russell Square Butte, used by the famous Montana artist in several of his paintings. Geologically speaking, this is a large laccolith, an intrusion of igneous rock formed as a blister of magma between layers of sedimentary rock. Meriwether Lewis's writings of July 15, 1805, noted, *"... we have now passed Fort Mountain on our right it appears to be about ten miles distance."* From his description of it being flat topped and steep on all sides, it is certain he was describing the same formation.

On July 18, Lewis mentioned, *"we passed the entrance a beautifull river 80 yards wide which falls in a Lard. (left side) Which in honour of Mr. Roberts Smith secretary of the navy we called Smiths River. This stream meanders through a most lovely valey to the S.E. for about 25 miles when it enters the Rocky mountains and is concealed from our view."* The Smith River, one of Montana's favorite for fly fishing and floating, works its way out of the Little Belt Mountains and then steers west to the Missouri near the hamlet of Ulm. A line of the Great Northern Railway came through in 1887 and what was once part of a ranch established by Bill Ulm became a town. Next door to Ulm sits Ulm Pishkun State Monument. An interpretive center tells the story of the many tepee rings found there and how tribes used the buffalo jump.

The Great Falls of the Missouri

Closing in on the city of Great Falls, a succession of soon-to-be-met dams causes the river to slow and relinquish its freedom to the act of creating power. No longer looking like a big river, it now takes on the appearance of a lake. One of the large inlets is even called Broadwater Bay.

This segment of the river was highly significant in the in the adventures of Lewis and Clark. During their 1804–1805 winter encampment at Fort Mandan, near present-day Bismarck, North Dakota, the Corps learned from the Hidatsa Indians that one of the principal landmarks along the water route to the Rocky Mountains was a *"great falls."*

In accordance with Lewis and Clark's time, we have been and will continue to tell their story backward ... this trip is downriver and the Expedition went against the current. Hopefully, this won't cause too much confusion for the reader.

On the south side of Great Falls, the first site is the White Bear Islands, labeled by Captain Clark in reference to the many grizzly bears inhabiting the area. The islands served as the base for the Upper Portage Camp during the very difficult traverse around the falls.

The Missouri River winds through the Gates of the Mountains.
RICK AND SUSIE GRAETZ

When Lewis and Clark came through this country, giant grizzlies were yet prairie animals. The islands not only served a feast of washed up buffalo carcasses for the bears, but the sand was soft, enabling them to easily excavate winter dens alongside the cottonwood trees.

The location of the Upper Portage Camp is still visible today, although time has silted in the channel that existed between it and the island they used for storage. The former riverbed is a very obvious depression running through a hay field. A lone cottonwood stands on the edge of what was once the riverbank.

Downriver from the islands on the west edge of Great Falls, the Sun River, another Hidatsa landmark, enters the now lake-like Missouri. Lewis's entry for June 14, 1805, included, "*I determined to procede ... convinced that it was the river the Indians call 'medicine'* (Sun)."

Five barriers: Black Eagle, Rainbow, Cochran, Ryan and Morony dams, all within 12 miles of each other, have obliterated the wondrous beauty Lewis described on June 13, 1805. After questioning whether or not the Corps had made the right decision concerning the Marias River not being the Missouri and that they were following the correct waterway, Lewis was desperately searching for the falls the Hidatsa had foretold of "*... whin my ears were saluted with the agreeable sound of a fall of water and advancing a little further I saw the spray arrise above the plain like a collumn of smoke ... which soon began to make a roaring too tremendous to be mistaken for any cause short of the great falls of the Missouri.*" Lewis clambered down a steep cliff in order "*to gaze on this is sublimely grand specticle ... the grandest sight I ever beheld.*"

▲ An old boat stands watch over Holter Lake.
RICK AND SUSIE GRAETZ

The Gates of the Mountains looking downriver.
RICK AND SUSIE GRAETZ

▲ The Missouri River out of Craig.
RICK AND SUSIE GRAETZ

▶ Near Cascade, the Missouri River and the Adel Mountains.
RICK AND SUSIE GRAETZ

Struck by a feeling of complete inadequacy to put into words the power and splendor of the sight before him, Lewis wished for the talent of an artist *"that I might be enabled to give to the enlightened world some just idea of this truly magnificent and sublimely grand object ... to give the world some faint idea of an object which at this moment fills me with such pleasure and astonishment, and which of it's kind I will venture to ascert is second to but one in the known world."* Being so overwhelmed, he set camp on the bank below the falls, later greatly diminished by Ryan Dam.

The next day, Lewis, headed off alone to scout the river above the falls. A quick five miles brought him to an unexpected second water cascade he named Crooked Falls. Then being led by *"a tremendous roaring above me,"* Lewis was awed by the scene of another "*great cataract*" that "*rivals for glory*" the one *"which I had discovered yesterday."* This once-glorious Rainbow Falls has been robbed of much of her splendor by the construction of Rainbow Dam. Almost immediately, Lewis stumbled onto another waterfall, no longer visible, having become jaded he explained *"in any other neighborhood but this, such a cascade would probably be extolled for it's beauty and magniffcence, but here I passed it by with but little attention ... At a distance of 2½ miles I arrived at another cataract of 26 feet ... below this falls at a little distance a beautiful little Island ... is situated about the middle of the river. In this Island on a Cottonwood tree an Eagle has placed her nest."* Another landmark complete with the noble bird's abode, just as the Hidatsa had described it!

The landmark's present-day name came more than 70 years later when Thomas P. Roberts, a railway engineer doing survey work while viewing the falls, was nearly attacked by a black eagle. Upon noticing the bird's nest in a cottonwood tree on an island below the thundering curtain of water, he recalled Lewis's mention of the same, and thought it fitting to christen the site Black Eagle Falls.

Somehow, something had been lost in the translation at Fort Mandan that past winter. Initially, from the information given by the Hidatsa, the captains assumed there would be just one falls and that it would only take a half-day to get around it. With a total of five major falls each separated by rapids, obviously the portage was going to take much longer.

On the 16th of June 1805, Captain Clark, with an extremely ill Sacajawea accompanying him, halted below the confluence of Belt Creek and the Missouri ("*portage creek*" to the Expedition), setting up what would become the base camp for their month-long assault around the *"great falls."* As part of Lewis's effort to cure the young mother, he used the water of a sulphur spring that is located across the Missouri from the mouth of Belt Creek and called Sacajawea or Sulphur Springs. The actual area of the Lower Portage Camp may be glimpsed looking downriver from Sulphur Springs toward a wide flat spot on the opposite shore. Owing to the rock outcrops on either side of the river, it is doubtful the channel has changed much with time. And the rapids Lewis details in his journal are still in place.

To make the portage, the men ascended Belt Creek and crossed the prairie near the present location of Malmstrom Air Force Base, hauling the boats to the southwest edge of Great Falls. They then followed Box Elder Creek ("*Willow Run*" in the journals) to the White Bear Islands and the Upper Portage Camp on the Missouri, a distance of about 18 miles.

Less than two miles below Black Eagle Dam, the world's *"shortest river,"* the Roe, extends to the Missouri from its source at Giant Springs. A sign placed by the Lincoln School fifth-grade class of 1987–1988 reads: *"The Roe River is the world's shortest river, having an average length of 201 feet, as recognized by the* Guinness Book of World Records. *Lewis and Clark were the first white people to see the river in 1805. The name "Roe" means fish eggs and comes from its proximity to the State Fish Hatchery."* The spring is part of the 3,400-acre Giant Springs State Park, which stretches for 14.5 miles along the Missouri at Great Falls.

The springs themselves are a wonderful natural phenomenon. Drs. Dave Alt and Don Hyndman, University of Montana geology professors, and authors of Roadside Geology of Montana, explain that "*... enormous volumes of water well up through fractures in the Kootenai sandstone and pour into the river. The great flow of these springs poses an interesting problem because the sandstone does not contain nearly enough open space to produce water in such quantity.*

"It seems likely that the water discharging from Giant Springs must be rising from the Madison Limestone, which lies several hundred feet below the surface. Limestones are the usual source of such large springs because they commonly contain caverns capable of conducting an enormous flow. If the Madison Limestone is indeed the source of Giant Springs, then the water probably comes from the Little Belt Mountains about 35 miles south east of Great Falls. That is the closest area where the Madison Limestone comes to the surface."

Paris Gibson of Minnesota read of the wonder of the *"great falls"* in the journals of Lewis and Clark and in 1880, he traveled to Montana to view them for himself. Rather than admiring the thundering cataracts as the captains had, Gibson felt that the water simply running over the falls was a waste and saw the possibility of dollars and power being generated instead. Gibson knew he would be able to persuade his friend Jim Hill, architect of the Great Northern Railway, to send a rail line to his city.

Young Paris returned to the falls again in 1882 and filed for ownership of the land that would grow to be Great Falls. In the summer of 1884, he set about building the town site and by 1887, the Montana Central Railway arrived, linking the city with mining camps and other towns in southwest Montana.

As Butte's Anaconda Company grew, new places with cheap power were needed to produce copper from Butte's ore. Gibson's new city by the cascades had all the right ingredients. A smelter was built on the north side of the river and a dam was constructed to supply the needed electricity. Black Eagle was the first of the magnificent falls to go under. The other dams fell in place over time.

Solid and staid, the grown-up city of Great Falls is the anchor of Montana's best grain growing region, The Golden Triangle. While agriculture rules the economy, the city is filled with art museums and historical venues, the kind of town one would like to raise a family in.

After managing Morony, the last of the dams, the Missouri will travel 32 miles, for the most part out of sight of roads and people, to Fort Benton. When it finds Benton, the river will have journeyed 245 miles from its origin and lost 1,386 feet in elevation.

Sixteen miles before reaching Fort Benton, the river passes the Carter Ferry, the first of three commuter boats serving backcountry roads and used mainly by ranchers and farmers. Working off a cable system, the ferries are rudimentary barges with a small engine house on one side. A person needing service presses a buzzer alerting the operator in his home and then awaits his cruise across the water.

The Virgelle Ferry at Virgelle and Coal Banks Landing is 39 miles below Fort Benton, and the McClelland operation crosses 64 miles downriver from Virgelle. The Carter and Virgelle boats are

Charlie Russell's Square Butte between Ulm and Cascade.
RICK AND SUSIE GRAETZ

A thunderstorm rolls through Great Falls.
RICK AND SUSIE GRAETZ

The Great Falls of the Missouri.
RICK AND SUSIE GRAETZ

near regularly traveled roads while McClelland isn't close to anywhere. It crosses the Missouri in a very remote segment of the Upper Missouri River Breaks National Monument.

FORT BENTON — MONTANA'S BIRTH PLACE

Of all the towns that touch the Missouri, Fort Benton is arguably the most historically significant and deserving of attention.

Just south of Fort Benton at a sweeping, open bend, the mighty river comes into view from the highway. An interpretive site, high above the river's west flank, looks down on cultivated land cradled by the waterway's curve. From 1845 until 1846, this was the location of an American Fur Company trading post, Fort Lewis, predecessor of Fort Benton. Winter ice jams and spring floods made access to the fort difficult so a new location was selected three miles downriver. The first residents moved there in the autumn of 1846, giving birth to what would become Montana. In 1847, the log buildings were dismantled and floated to the young community.

The reconstructed and relocated structure and settlement was named Fort Clay. On Christmas day 1850, the name was changed to Fort Benton in honor of Senator Thomas Hart Benton, a patron of the American Fur Company. A lucrative fur trade sustained the town through the 1850s.

The Missouri River Steamboat Era, lasting from 1860 until 1888, gave this riverbank community new life at a time when the fur trade was dwindling. On July 2, 1860, carried by the high waters of that summer, the Chippewa from St. Louis was the first boat to reach Fort Benton. A steamer made an attempt in 1859, but was forced to stop 12 miles short of Benton as the river was falling and they were short of fuel. This, the oldest continuing settlement in the state, became the head of navigation of the lifeline to the soon-to-be Montana Territory. Territorial status was granted in May, 1864.

It wasn't long before Fort Benton became a boisterous *"Old West"* town of legend. As Winfield Stocking wrote, *"Although it continued to be a mere village in size, in a commercial way it was the Chicago of the plains. It was the door through which all the gold hunters, adventurers, speculators, traders, land-seekers, big game hunters, fugitives from justice, desperadoes and all the bad Indians on the top of the earth entered the Northwest."* A sign on the levee states that the street along the river was *"The bloodiest block in the west."*

Gold discoveries in western Montana created a rush that attracted hordes miners. The charge for the glittering metal started in July 1862 with the territory's first major gold strike on Grasshopper Creek in Bannack. The uncovering of gold there was followed in May 1863 by the find in Alder Gulch near Virginia City and then Last Chance Gulch in Helena in 1864. An estimated 10,000 people made the journey along with countless tons of freight; and Missouri River steamboats were the most practical way to get here. The trip to Fort Benton from St. Louis took 60 days and cost about $150.

From the time the ice melted in the spring until the river froze in the fall, the one and one-half-mile-long levee at Fort Benton was piled with goods headed for the gold camps of southwest Montana. *"All trails lead out of Fort Benton"* was a familiar statement in those days. The young settlement was the anchor of the 625-mile-long Mullan Road that, when completed in 1862, led to Walla Walla, Washington. Travelers heading out of town used stage lines and bull and mule trains.

The steamboat era brought about 600 boats up the Missouri. The years 1860–1869 witnessed the highest flow of passage. During the 1867 season, 71 steamboats made it up the river. After 1869, traffic dwindled some each year. The advent of the railroads into Montana and to Fort Benton in September 1887 put an end to use of the river as a primary source of transportation and trade.

Settlers had followed the gold seekers upriver on the sternwheelers, but when the silver spike for the railroad was driven near Fort Benton, this period also came to an end. Now, would-be homesteaders rode the steel rails to claim land along the Missouri.

Fort Benton is one of the most fascinating and, especially when seen in the spring, summer and fall months, attractive towns in Montana. The cottonwood-lined Missouri River flows peacefully along a well-maintained levee area of commercial buildings and old homes. It's hard to imagine that this quiet, agricultural town was as rough and raucous as the stories tell. But the sights and sounds of history past are part of what makes Fort Benton so special today. The townsfolk have gone out of their way to preserve important reminders of a way of life that once was.

Fort Benton's pride and joy, the refurbished Grand Union, Montana's oldest operating hotel, holds court along the park-like riverbank. This historic landmark was originally opened on November 1, 1882, and as one of the signs along the levee states, *"U.S. Army officers, Canadian Mounties, trappers, miners, traders, river captains, stockman, missionaries, Indian agents and road agents rubbed shoulders in the Grand Union's lobby, spacious dining room and adjourned to its well stocked bar for the relaxation due the frontiersman at a weary journey's end."*

Rising from a sandstone bluff north of town, Signal Point was once used by spotters to sight steamboats chugging upriver eight miles away. Word then went out to the townsfolk that a steamer was *"round the bend!"* Today from Signal Point and other places on this high perch, one can get a great view of the big Missouri and Fort Benton.

From here on down for the next 300 miles, the river will maneuver through some of the most storied and magnificent prairie landscape in the West. Save for tiny Loma, guardian of the Marias — a major tributary, towns are removed from any contact with the river and the importance of the terrain extends much farther from the waterway than it does upstream.

Upper Missouri River Breaks National Monument

In October 1976, 149 miles of the fabled Missouri River — from Fort Benton downstream to the Fred Robinson Bridge — and the adjacent 135,350 acres of land gained designation as a National Wild and Scenic River. On January 18, 2001, it was granted National Monument status and the acreage was increased to 374,976.

Heading north and east from Fort Benton, mile zero in the Monument, the river flows calmly. Even the once noxious, steamboat-catching rapids such as Deadman and Dauphine hardly make a ripple on its surface. Silently, it passes through fertile river bottoms past some of the West's most remote and least inhabited country. Incredible rock formations, austere badlands and magnificent river canyon and prairie scenery, coupled with the historical lure of the place, bring floaters back many times over.

▲ The old bridge over the Missouri at Fort Benton.
RICK AND SUSIE GRAETZ

◀ Sunrise on the Missouri River near Ulm.
JOHN LAMBING

The original site of Fort Lewis, predecessor to Fort Benton.

RICK AND SUSIE GRAETZ

The great Indian Nations knew the river first. West of the White Cliffs area, located about 51 water miles from Fort Benton, was the homeland of the powerful Blackfeet. Below this terrain, the Gros Ventre, Assiniboine and Cree claimed hunting rights.

Lewis and Clark came into what is now the National Monument on May 24, 1805, making camp three miles upstream from today's Fred Robinson Bridge (Mile 149 of the Monument). Pulling the heavily laden boats upriver, often in deep water, and walking through mud, the men of the Corps of Discovery toiled to ascend the *"Big Muddy."* The explorers exited today's Monument segment of the Missouri on June 13, 1805.

The record of their days spent in this 149-mile section, captures some of the most noteworthy moments of the entire Expedition.

On June 2, 1805, the Corps camped at the mouth of the Marias, about 22 river miles from Benton. In 1950, a flood diverted the course of the Marias River forcing it to enter the Missouri nearly one mile farther upstream, thereby altering a physical location in history. The former channel is still visible along the cliffs near Loma.

Up until June 2, 1805, the information supplied to the Expedition by the Hidatsa Indians during their winter 1804–1805 encampment proved to be most accurate. On that date however, the Corps encountered something not shown on the crude maps they possessed. The Missouri they had been following for so many months appeared now to split into a north and south fork. The Indians had made no mention of another major waterway coming from the north after the Milk River. They only specified that the explorers would meet a great waterfall, and then soon thereafter the river would enter the mountains.

The two leaders were fairly sure the south fork was the Missouri, but the crew was convinced otherwise. Joseph Whitehouse, a member of the Corps, noted in his journal on June 3, *"our officers and all the men differ in their opinions which river to take."* Characteristic of their excellent leadership, the captains agreed to explore both branches so all would be assured.

Lewis on June 3, 1805, scripted, *"to this end an investigation of both streams was the first thing to be done ... accordingly we dispatched two light canoes with three men in each up those streams; we also sent out several small parties by land with instructions to penetrate the country as far as they conveniently can permitting themselves time to return this evening and indeavour if possible to discover the distant bearing of those rivers by ascending the rising grounds ... Capt. C. & myself stroled out it to the top of the hights in the fork of these rivers from whence we had an extensive and most inchanting view ... to the south we saw a range of lofty mountains"* (most likely the Highwoods, east of Great Falls).

The *"top of the hights"* the captains climbed is reached via a dirt road just south of Loma off Hwy 87 and is now marked as Decision Point.

After the return of the scouting parties, there was still much uncertainty. It was then decided to explore farther, Clark would follow the south fork (Missouri) and Lewis the north (Marias).

June 4, 1805, the two groups separated. It didn't take Clark long to deduce that the south fork was the correct way to go. Lewis meanwhile, traveled 60 to 70 miles up the north fork before coming to the same conclusion. On June 6, 1805, he wrote, *"I now became well convinced that this branch of the Missouri had its direction too much to the north for our rout to the Pacific, and therefore*

▲ The historic Grand Union Hotel, built in Fort Benton in 1882.
RICK AND SUSIE GRAETZ

◀ Decision Point at the confluence of the Missouri and Marias Rivers.
RICK AND SUSIE GRAETZ

▲ The town of Loma stands near the confluence of the Missouri and Marias rivers.
RICK AND SUSIE GRAETZ

▶ The Marias River.
JOHN LAMBING

determined to return." So assured that the river he was following was not the Missouri, on June 8, Lewis named it Maria's River for his cousin.

In any dissertation of Montana's rivers, the Marias deserves some coverage because of its historical significance.

South of Cut Bank and north of Valier, in a rugged broken part of the prairie, where badlands and sandstone formations prevail, Cut Bank Creek and the Two Medicine River join forces to jumpstart the Marias. The Two Medicine River begins deep in the Rocky Mountain Front in an area sacred to the Blackfeet Nation. Cut Bank Creek also takes its initial waters from the Rocky Mountain Front, just off of the Hudson Bay Divide in Glacier National Park.

The Marias flows for approximately 170 miles twisting and turning through deep canyons and a rolling, sculptured prairie landscape as it forges its way toward the Missouri.

Two miles before the confluence, the Teton River, itself a product of the Rocky Mountain Front, joins in and together they flow under the U.S. Hwy 87 bridge at Loma and give up their waters to the Missouri.

On May 31, 1805, the Corps spent the night at one of the Upper Missouri's most scenic campsites, the White Cliffs and Eagle Creek (Mile 55.7). Lewis penned these poetic words:

"*... the men are compelled to be in the water even to their armpits, and the water is yet very could ... added to this the banks and bluffs along which they are obliged to pass are so slippery and the mud so tenacious that they are unable to wear their mockersons, and in that situation draging the heavy burthen of a canoe and walking acasionally for several hundred yards over the sharp fragments of rocks ... in short their labour is incredibly painfull and great, yet those faithful fellows bear it without a murmur ... The hills and river Clifts which we passed today exhibit a most romantic appearance. The bluffs of the river rise to the hight of from 2 to 300 feet and in most places nearly perpendicular; they are formed of remarkable white sandstone ... The water in the course of time in decending from those hills and plains on either side of the river has trickled down the soft sand clifts and woarn it into a thousand grotesque figures, which with the help of a little immagination ... are made to represent eligant ranges of lofty freestone buildings, having their parapets well stocked with statuary; collumns of various sculpture both grooved and plain, are also seen supporting long galleries in front of those buildings; in other places ... we see the remains or ruins of eligant buildings ... the tops of the collumns did not the less remind us of some of those large stone buildings in the U. States ... as we passed on it seemed as if those seens of visionary inchantment would never have an end; for here it is too that nature presents to the view, of the traveler vast ranges of walls of tolerable workmanship, so perfect indeed are those walls that I should have thought that nature had attempted here to rival the human art of masonry had I not, recollected that she had first began her work.*"

Eagle Creek, in addition to being one of the most picturesque locations along the river and a Lewis and Clark campsite, holds remnants of bison drive lines, tipi rings, rock cairns and flint knapping workshops; all marvelous reminders of the presence of the area's earliest residents.

After the Corps of Discovery, owing to Indian resistance, whites didn't show up here again until 1830 when they were lured, in spite of the dangers, by the fur business. In the summer of 1831, Fort Piegan Trading Post was established at the confluence of the Marias and Missouri rivers. Only lasting through the winter, it was replaced several miles upriver by Fort McKenzie.

Brulé Bottoms — a sight that artist Carl Bodmer painted in 1833.

RICK AND SUSIE GRAETZ

Prince Maximilian, a German scientist, came to the McKenzie trading post in 1833, to study the Indians and collect animal and plant specimens. Artist Karl Bodmer, who accompanied him, showed the world through his paintings what the upper Missouri looked like.

Built late in 1832 to trade with the Piegans, Bloods and Blackfeet, the life of Fort McKenzie was cut short in January of 1844 when a party of young Blackfeet warriors returning from the Crow country asked admittance to the fort and were refused by a hotheaded Frenchman, Francois A. Chardon, and his lieutenant, Alexander Harvey. The warriors retaliated by stealing and killing some of the fort's livestock. A well-armed party pursued them, but in the fray, Chardon's negro slave was killed and scalped. Vowing revenge, they loaded the fort's cannon with 150 or so lead bullets, aimed it at the approach to the main gate and waited for the next Indian trading party.

In February, a small band of either Piegans or Bloods arrived to trade. Before Harvey could put fire to the cannon, Chardon fired his rifle killing one chief, the other Indians scattered. Five were hit and two were killed, although some stories say as many as 30 were killed instantly. Further trading at the fort was impossible. Chardon and company moved downriver to the mouth of the Judith on April 5, 1844. Fort McKenzie was then burned either by whites or Indians, and to this day the site is known as Brulé (burned) Bottom.

Many other landmarks throughout the Monument sector of the Missouri have significant meaning in the annals of the river. Coal Banks Landing and Woodhawk Creek were places where steamboats picked up the fuel they needed from the woodhawkers who lived lonely and threatened lives along the river's edge. Markers such as Steamboat, LaBarge and Pilot rocks, were given their names by the big boat captains.

At Cow Island, when the water was too low to make it to Fort Benton, many a steamboat had to unload their freight and let wagons carry it to the town. This spot was also a major ford for Indians and bison. In the fall of 1877, military supplies had been unloaded on the island. Chief Joseph and his starving band of Nez Perce crossed the Missouri here on their flight to Canada. After failing to peacefully negotiate with the small military guard troop for much needed supplies, took what they needed and burned the rest.

The physical geography of this river country is diverse. Undulating hills, table top rims and fertile bottom lands make up the landscape from Fort Benton to Coal Banks, a myriad of coulees and imaginative rock formations stretch from the Eagle Creek and the White Cliffs/Rocks area on through and past Hole-in-the-Wall, then distinctive badlands, steep slopes and wide banks accent the skyline to Fred Robinson Bridge. Here and there, stands of riverside and island cottonwoods add to the river's beauty.

Relief from the water level to the upper rims varies from 400 feet near Fort Benton to more than 1,000 feet in the badlands and breaks areas below Judith Landing. And depths of the river vary greatly, ranging from a few inches to 15 feet deep.

The White Cliffs/White Rocks country shows some of the most interesting and photogenic scenes on the Upper Missouri. The area's white sandstone crumbles easily while the yellowish-red colored material found here is harder and therefore more erosion resistant. Thus the white pillars with the tinged caps are formed. Toadstools and thin sandstone walls, common to this area, were created by water and wind erosion.

Residents of Giant Springs at Great Falls.
RICK AND SUSIE GRAETZ

Some of the Monument's farthest downstream reaches are actually small desert environments. The badlands, or "*mauvaises terres*" as the French trappers called them, are formed when fire or some other disruption destroys the plant cover that normally protects the soil from being eroded. Rainwater hits the denuded surface compacting it and seeds can't take hold, then runoff forms gullies and soon, strange looking formations appear.

The namesake of the National Monument, the river breaks, are sculptured by the erosive action of water on the soil and soft rocks underlying the surface. Small gulches and deep canyons are cut out of the higher landscape as streams of rainwater and snowmelt find their path to the river. The resulting terrain is rough, wild and spectacular.

Weather patterns throughout the Monument sector as well as all along this historic waterway vary widely. Summer can bring searing dry heat with temperatures exceeding 100 degrees, violent thunderstorms, heavy rain, and even hail and snow. In winter, north winds whip up ferocious blizzards and the thermometer may lower to 50 below zero, or warm southwest winds can make a January day feel like spring. May and June, although sometimes wet, bring the beauty of wildflowers and green to the landscape and in late September and October, the gold, orange and red of the shoreline and coulees present a wondrous show against a deep blue and cloudless sky.

▲ Virgelle near Coal Banks Landing on the Missouri.
RICK AND SUSIE GRAETZ

Vegetation is diverse and includes groves of cottonwoods, ash, box elder, willows, conifers, grasses, sagebrush, greasewood and low lying riparian growth.

The present lack of cottonwood and willow regeneration is under discussion by the Bureau of

Land Management, the federal agency charged with management of the river. Silt, carried on the faster, high water brought on by uncontrolled runoff from spring floods, is required to prepare cottonwood seed beds. Because of upstream dams, this no longer happens. In the winter, ice jams occur and scour out what seedlings do manage to grow.

Hot weather grazing along the banks also leads to the destruction of newly sprouted cottonwoods. This is an issue the BLM is attempting to work out with local ranchers. One of the possible solutions is to provide solar powered pumps for water tanks on higher ground. Some operators are voluntarily pulling their stock out of the area during mid-summer.

Wildlife earn a good living in the embankments, coulees and canyons of the protected Monument lands. Sixty species of mammals, 230 different kinds of birds and 20 breeds of amphibians and reptiles make this tract of the upper Missouri River and its environs their home. Mule deer, as well as sharp-tailed grouse, are abundant on the slopes and coulees, while the rolling areas above the river bottoms make good habitat for antelope and sage grouse. Golden eagles, prairie falcons and hawks perch and nest in the cliffs above the river.

Forty-nine varieties of fish have been identified, including gold-eye, sauger, northern pike, sturgeon and walleye. The Upper Missouri River has one of the six remaining paddlefish populations left in the nation.

Even before the lower end of the National Monument is reached, the next great Missouri River prize, the Charles M. Russell National Wildlife Refuge establishes its upper limit. For ten miles, the Missouri bears the flags of both public treasures to Kipp Landing at the Fred Robinson Bridge.

Incidentally, the bridge was dedicated to Fred Robinson, who was the force behind getting the bridge built. Finished in 1959, it allows U.S. Hwy 191 to span the Missouri.

Charles M. Russell National Wildlife Refuge

It's an uncommon geography: at once stark, beautiful, imposing and inviting, this Charles M. Russell National Wildlife Refuge. Time has left most of the remarkable landscape with the same appearance as when the indigenous peoples hunted and did battle here. And while some of the wildlife species have disappeared, notably bison and grizzly bears, other animals, including elk and bighorn sheep are coming back strong.

The CMR, as it is commonly referred to, occupies a large swath of Montana's northeast quadrant and is in the center of some of the least inhabited country in the United States. The 1.1-million-acre refuge straddles a section of the flowing Missouri River and takes in the rugged Missouri Breaks, wild prairie grasslands and the 250,000-acre Fort Peck Lake with its 1,600 miles of shoreline. From the western boundary 10 miles upstream of the Fred Robinson Bridge near Grand Island, a canoe will cover 150 miles by the time it reaches the spillway of Fort Peck Dam and the eastern perimeter of the refuge. The U.S. Fish and Wildlife Service manages this animal haven.

In many places, the CMR's broken and rough terrain is difficult to negotiate. Nearly 80 percent of the place is made up of steep ridges and a labyrinth of eroded coulees. In wet weather, the underlying shale and clay turns to gumbo, and travel, either by vehicle or on foot, becomes almost impossible.

The mix of landforms of the CMR is impressive. Table-topped uplands give way to rugged ravines, wide and precipitous canyons (some 1,000-feet deep) and spectacular badlands. This much-dissected expanse of ground has been broken by flows of water, such as Seven Blackfeet Creek, Devils Creek, Snow Creek, Hell Creek, the Musselshell River and many smaller, more intermittent creeks. Hence the term *"river breaks."*

Elevations and relief are low by Montana standards, but when looking up at some of the high points from the bottom of a gulch, the slopes appear as tough to climb as any mountain. When Fort Peck Lake is at full pool, the lowest elevation on the refuge is 2,246 feet. One of the loftiest spots is 3,241 feet high on a divide just above the east side of Seven Blackfeet Creek, close to the center of the CMR.

An open forest of Rocky Mountain juniper, Douglas fir and ponderosa pines covers close to one-third of the refuge. Ponderosa, the dominant tree, is a stunted version of the taller pines that grow west of Montana's Continental Divide. Wildlife use these woodlands for security, and the timber also protects the fragile soil from erosion. Sagebrush and grasslands intersperse the trees and comprise almost 60 percent of the land. Riparian habitats are found along the banks of the Missouri River and many of the smaller creeks.

When flying above the CMR, it is interesting to note that the tree coverage is far more extensive on the south side of the Missouri than the north. On the south, the forests can extend up to 10 miles inland, while in the north they are seldom much more than two or three miles in width. This is especially true of the country east of UL Bend. The slopes ascending from the south banks of the river accumulate more moisture, have better soils and provide a more suitable environment for tree growth than the breaks north of the Missouri.

Fox Hills sandstone and the Hell Creek geologic formations dominate the CMR beyond the southern edge of Fort Peck Lake and the Missouri. The north side of the waterways was glaciated about 15,000 years ago by continental ice sheets flowing into northeast Montana out of Canada. These glaciers pushed the Missouri River south out of its old channel to its present location. The Milk River now occupies the former Missouri River bed. Scouring glacial ice also removed the quality earth, exposing the fine textured clay-like Bearpaw shale, which is less conducive to producing vegetation.

Through the centuries, much of the landscape in the southeastern environs of the refuge has been highly eroded by exposure to wind and water. The mudstone and other soils that have been uncovered contain ancient marine life and dinosaur bones. The area continues to yield some of the richest records of prehistoric life in the world.

More than two million acres of mostly public land managed by the Bureau of Land Management surround the Charles M. Russell refuge. Primitive roads cross this BLM land and lead to the CMR.

Unlike most of the refuge, this outlying terrain is predominantly rolling prairie broken by shallow coulees and occasional buttes. Vegetation is mostly sagebrush, prickly pear cactus and native prairie grass. Rocky Mountain juniper is widely scattered throughout. Drainages that make up the river breaks of the CMR get their start in small draws and deeper gulches of this higher ground beyond the preserve.

Eagle Creek and the White Cliffs of the Missouri — a Lewis and Clark campsite of May 31, 1805.

RICK AND SUSIE GRAETZ

The beginning of the White Cliffs in the Upper Missouri River Breaks National Monument.

RICK AND SUSIE GRAETZ

Citadel Rock, landmark near the Hole in the Wall area.
RICK AND SUSIE GRAETZ

Castle Rock holds court over the Missouri.
RICK AND SUSIE GRAETZ

Regions of the CMR

The Missouri River flows freely in the western reaches of the Charles M. Russell National Wildlife Refuge. Its meanders have created wide river bottoms and fertile ground for large stands of cottonwoods, willows and ash trees that provide good white-tailed deer environment. The slopes of the hills in this section are less angular than those farther east, and getting around on foot is easier here than it is downstream.

Large drainages, such as Rock Creek and Sipary Ann Creek, flowing south to the Missouri River from the Little Rocky Mountains and nearby terrain, have dissected the prairie in the northwestern province of the CMR into a north-south pattern of ridges and coulees. South of the Missouri, waterways, including Sand Creek, Two Calf Creek and Crooked Creek flow east to west. Primitive roads follow many of the ridges above these creeks allowing good access to the protected lands.

In several places on the south side, steep winding roads descend to the river flood plain. As for the north fringe of the river, a road, starting at Hwy 191, parallels the Missouri for about 14 miles. Other byways head north beyond the river toward the Little Rockies and Malta.

In this area, just beyond the Sand Creek Wildlife Station, from a ridge high above the south rim of the Missouri's canyon, the horizons, on a clear day, extend for up to 100 miles. Many of north central Montana's *"island mountain ranges,"* including the Little Rockies, Big Snowies, Judith, Bear Paw and Moccasin are visible.

Primary access to the western part of the refuge is from above both sides of the Fred Robinson Bridge and Hwy 191.

About 18 miles east of the bridge, the Missouri's progress is slowed as the waters of Fort Peck Lake begin to backup. The flood plain disappears and the lake covers the bottomlands. When the water level drops, mud flats appear and the old channel takes shape. At one time, these bottoms provided extensive stands of cottonwoods and riparian land covered by lush vegetation. Lewis and Clark found bison, elk and grizzly bears as they moved along the shore of the river.

From this point east, the river corridor begins to widen. Both sides of the waterway consist of countless coulees and open ponderosa pine forests. As the ebb of water nears a big bend known as UL Bend, the surface on the north side becomes noticeably flatter and void of trees. Low hills separated by shallow draws blend with level ground; views are distant. As far as the eye can see in any direction is one of the most widespread and least disturbed short-grass prairies in the nation. And it supports one of the world's largest networks of prairie dog colonies. The existence of such great numbers of black-tailed prairie dogs on the UL Bend is sustaining the comeback of the black-footed ferret, an endangered and rare mammal. Ferrets need these prairie diggers to survive; they live in their burrows and prey on them. The *"Bend"* is also a good area to view the colorful mating rituals of sage and sharp-tail grouse.

The pinch-necked, horseshoe-shaped landform that makes up the lower portion of the UL Bend region is about seven miles long, one mile across at its narrowest point and about 13 miles around. Steamboats plying the Missouri in the mid 1800s let their passengers off on one side so they could walk across and get their *"land legs"* back after having spent many days on-board. The boats would continue around and retrieve them on the other side of the peninsula.

The Marias River.

RICK AND SUSIE GRAETZ

The UL Bend National Wildlife Refuge and UL Bend Wilderness are part of this remote area. Both are contiguous to and managed by the CMR through the U.S. Fish and Wildlife Service.

Headwatering in the Castle Mountains of western Montana, the historic Musselshell River winds through its valley from the south reaching the Missouri across from the tip of the UL Bend.

East of UL Bend and the Musselshell, the country gets even rougher, the reservoir widens and more bays sculpture the shoreline on both sides of the lake. This is the mid-section of the CMR. Mickey and Brandon buttes, each about 2,900 feet in elevation and home to bighorn sheep, are landmarks on the north side of the water. On the same side of the river, but farther east, rising to 3,140 feet, Iron Stake Ridge, the southern most reach of the Larb Hills, stands out. South of the river and lake, the sharp divides above Devils Creek, Herman Ridge and Seven Blackfeet reach above some of the most rugged landscape on the CMR. Relief is from 500 to 1,000 feet high.

The mass of the Larb Hills and the untamed geography across the river presents perhaps the most dramatic and beautiful display of upland prairie topography on the continent. Both sides of the river and lake in this span of the refuge create territory for mule deer, elk, bighorn sheep and antelope as well as smaller critters. Here, nature also displays a fascinating collection of picturesque rock configurations ... castles, monuments, towers, arches — all created by differential erosion, such as harder rock sitting atop a softer eroding stone pedestal.

Beyond the mouth of Seven Blackfeet, the inlets on the south broaden and become longer; now there is no mistaking the lake for a river. North of Jordan, the popular recreation areas of Snow Creek and Hell Creek bays stretch south from the main body of water. The north side of the shoreline in this region is extremely irregular. Narrow points of land separate at least ten bays and flat-topped buttes accentuate the ground above them.

As the water spreads out and nears its widest expanse, the landforms on either side become more subdued. The highest hills are 2,500 feet to 2,600 feet above sea level; the relief is not much more than 100 feet. Because of the section's sparse tree cover, elk are scarce. This rolling prairie and open terrain is habitat for the speedy pronghorn antelope.

The eastern edge of the lake takes an abrupt and lengthy turn to the south of the main body of water. Dry Arm, called "*Big Dry Creek*" before the dam, stretches out for about 40 miles. This finger-shaped extension of Fort Peck Lake is greater in length by itself, than any other lake in the state.

Badlands make up much of the surface geology of the eastern part of this wildlife haven. Views here are austere and beautiful. The Sand Arroyo Badlands are the most distinguished of these dry land creations. Unusual and fascinating rock arrangements, many looking like dinosaur footprints suspended on pillars, are scattered throughout a desert-like environment. Made of sandstone, they too were created by wind blowing the finer material away from the rock, leaving the coarser stone standing above the surface.

Although the sunrise side of the CMR is the driest of all the preserve regions, in the Bobcat Creek drainage, pockets of perennial wet areas exist. Just below the surface soils, water moves laterally along impermeable coal seams and seeps out in some of the deeper coulees prompting the growth of green ash trees and other vegetation. In one coulee, aspens have taken hold and in another, black cottonwoods are growing. Usually found in cooler, wetter environs, it is rare for these two species of trees to be so far east of the mountains.

Hole in the Wall, a favorite hiking and camping area.

RICK AND SUSIE GRAETZ

North of Sand Arroyo, the relief begins to increase. The 3,000-foot Deadman's Butte, a promontory just beyond the eastern reaches of the Refuge, dominates the landscape. The summit provides sweeping views of the immense expanse of sky, water and land spread out to the south, west and north. On a clear day, it's possible to see a thousand square miles of prairie and river.

CMR History

The recorded history of the country now designated as the Charles M. Russell National Wildlife Refuge flows with the waters of the Missouri River.

Long before the first visitors and millions of years prior to the formation of the Missouri, other forms of life existed here. Evidence of this presence is found in the mudstones and other sedimentary formations that blanket the CMR. The Missouri River badlands of the refuge and beyond are producing new discoveries each year. Paleontologists have been provided with one of the world's most fertile fossil sites and an outdoor laboratory to help them understand the evolutionary process.

Tyrannosaurus rex, Triceratops, Albertosaurus, Mosasaurus (a marine reptile), aquatic duck-billed dinosaurs and other giant creatures roamed, fought and populated this preserve area. In 1902, one of the first T-rex fossils ever found was discovered near Jordan in the Cretaceous era badlands of Hell Creek. In 1990, the most complete T-rex ever, was unearthed here. Each year brings new finds, exciting information and enlightenment about what this land surrounding the Missouri was like more than 70 million years ago.

Indian tribes from the upper Midwest and farther east, were pushed west into this region by an expanding white population. By the late 1700s, a Plains Indian culture, centered on the movement of bison, had been established, along and beyond the big river.

The original Plains Indians who used these lands were the Shoshone, Flathead, Pend Oreille and Kootenai. Then the growing Blackfeet nation, especially the most feared Piegan Blackfeet, forced the others to the mountains. While the Blackfeet dominated this region, Assiniboine, Atsina (also known at the Gros Ventre of the Plains), Cree, Absaroka, Sioux and Gros Ventre also hunted here. The river was supposed to have divided the hunting grounds, but rarely did it stand in the way of trespass and many major battles were fought over hunting rights.

The first recorded documentation of this Charlie Russell Country began in 1805 with the journals of Lewis and Clark. In May of that year, they spent 16 days traveling up river through what is now the Charles M. Russell National Wildlife Refuge. Most of their campsites are presently under the waters of Fort Peck Reservoir, but three of the approximate locations are on the western end of the refuge and can be reached by primitive road.

On May 9, 1805, the Corps passed Big Dry Creek and camped near what is now Duck Creek. Lewis wrote, *"today we passed the bed of the most extraordinary river that I ever beheld. it is as wide as the Missouri is at this place or ½ a mile wide and not containing a single drop of runing water."*

Reaching the Musselshell River on May 20, they named it the *"Shell River."* Camping here for the night, Lewis penned, *"The hunters returned this evening and informed us that the country continued much the same in appearance as that we saw where we were or broken, and that about five*

▲ Igneous outcroppings amid sandstone in the Upper Missouri River Breaks National Monument.
RICK AND SUSIE GRAETZ

◀ Sunset on the cliffs above the Missouri.
RICK AND SUSIE GRAETZ

▲ Judith River near Judith Landing and its confluence with the Missouri.
RICK AND SUSIE GRAETZ

▸ Badlands on the Upper Missouri.
RICK AND SUSIE GRAETZ

miles ab[ov]e the mouth of shell river a handsome river of about fifty yards in width discharged itself into the shell river on the Stard (north*) or upper side; this stream we called Sah-ca-ger we-ah or bird woman's River after our interpreter the Snake woman."*

On May 22, the explorers set up camp just below CK Creek on the north shore of the Missouri. Clark noted in the journals, *"I walked out after dinner and assended a but[te] a few miles [off] to view the countrey, which I found roleing & of a verry rich stickey soil producing but little vegetation of any kind except the prickley pear, but little grass & that verry low."* Clark was probably observing the gumbo soil prevalent on the CMR when it rains.

Fur trappers and traders followed the Corps of Discovery on the Missouri. Activity was minimal until the late 1820s when larger organizations like the American Fur Company moved into the area and established trading posts. Traders labored against the currents of the river with loads of material for bartering, then floated downstream with heaps of furs secured from the Indians and trappers.

After Lewis and Clark and the trappers, and up until the 1880s when the steel rails entered the territory, the Missouri was the main route of travel into Montana. Today's wildlife refuge stretch of the Missouri and the lands on both sides of the water, were host to everyone who added to the tales and legends of *"the Wild West."* Rustlers, horse thieves, bank robbers, cattleman, vigilantes, cowboys, Native Americans, trappers, woodhawkers, wolfers, steamboat captains and the U.S. Calvary passed through or lived here for a short spell. Very few areas experienced as much of the history of the early American west as did this place.

As the water traffic increased, several riverfront settlements, such as Carroll in the western end of the refuge soon sprung up. At first a trading post, Carroll later became a steamboat landing that enjoyed brief prosperity during the low water years of 1874 and 1875. Freight and passengers were unloaded here to continue the journey west by land over the Carroll Trail to Helena. This good fortune ended when the return of high water allowed the steamboats once again to continue upriver to Fort Benton.

Rocky Point, in the western part of the Russell Wildlife Refuge, was a tough frontier town from the 1860s until the turn of the century. Serving legitimate ranchers and businessmen, as well as the thieves and outlaws, it became the rendezvous and center of trade for wood choppers, trappers, miners, cowboys, whiskey-traders and all manner of desperados, including the infamous Kid Curry and his gang. Rocky Point also served as a steamboat landing, with infantry companies occasionally stationed to guard government freight.

Remnants of Rocky Point, like those of Carroll and other riverbank towns, have been washed away, leaving little evidence of their one-time existence.

Perhaps the most fascinating time of the Old West and the Missouri River Breaks was in the early 1870s. Western Montana stockmen ventured into the lush river bottoms and tall grass of the north central part of the state. The land was unfenced and un-owned. Pioneer institutions — big outfits such as the DHS Ranch and the Circle C Ranch — ranged their livestock through what is now the CMR. And big cattle drives, up from Texas were brought north into the area to feed on the nutritional grasses.

Outlaws, rustlers and thieves took advantage of the open range and the somewhat easy practice of stealing horses and cattle. They had their favorite haunts and would hole up in the many coulees of the badlands until they could safely dispose of the stolen goods. These outlaws, and others on the

"Toadstools" in the Upper Missouri River Breaks National Monument.

RICK AND SUSIE GRAETZ

run from the law, hung out in places like Carroll, Rocky Point and Musselshell. Signs of their camps and the corrals that held stolen livestock can be seen in remote areas of the refuge.

In 1867, a northern Pony Express route came through what is now the Wildlife Refuge. Starting at Fort Union on the Missouri and close to today's Montana/North Dakota line, the trail follows Hwy 2, reaching the Missouri River again at Fort Peck at the eastern end of the CMR. Riders stayed on the north side of the Missouri until they reached Fort Hawley, on Hawley Creek west of the UL Bend. Here they crossed the Missouri and headed southwest to the Judith Mountains and Helena. Mail service on this route lasted for just one year.

The heyday of the wide-ranging cattle industry was about to come to an end. The tough winter of 1886–87 caused heavy livestock losses and began the decline of the big cattle operations. Life in the Missouri Breaks calmed.

Homesteaders, lured to the Montana plains by glowing railroad reports touting prospects of riches to be reaped from the soil and a 1909 liberal homestead law, began making inroads on the eastern Montana prairies. Some settled along the lush bottomlands of the Missouri River. For the most part, the lands that would eventually be set aside for the Charles M. Russell National Wildlife Refuge weren't suited for agriculture and the majority of homestead claims were made along the river. After 1910, almost every bottom with enough level ground to make farming worthwhile had been settled.

Small hamlets grew along the Missouri to serve those homesteaders who did settle in the Breaks. At one time, there were 16 post offices located throughout the river country.

At first, these newcomers did well with their crops. In 1917 though, drought set in and worsened over the next three years. This natural calamity, coupled with several severe recessions, extreme winter weather and isolation destroyed the dreams of many who came to settle in the soon-to-be CMR. Most were forced to leave their places to the wind and let nature reclaim the land. Postal locations such as Round Butte, Big Dry, Wilder, Trenton and Bervie all disappeared. Faint reminders of these earlier times are still found, but they are lost in the enormity of a mostly unspoiled territory

Only a few hardy folk stayed on, and they are the roots of today's big ranching operations. Those ranchers and farmers who were successful in establishing places along the river and withstood the drought were bought out by the U.S. Government in the 1930s as a prelude to the building of Fort Peck Dam.

With the completion of the dam 1940, the river behind it deepened and spread, covering the cottonwoods, floodplain and history alike. The smooth waters have brought a sense of tranquility to the land, drowning the voices of the past. But oftentimes, as the wind rustles across the grass and through the trees, very faintly, those voices can be heard.

From Fort Peck to The Yellowstone

At this point, the Missouri River hasn't seen a town since Loma, 281 miles ago. In 1876, near the site of today's Fort Peck Dam, Colonel Campbell Peck and Commander Durfee of the U.S. Army established an Indian Agency and a trading post for the Assiniboine and Sioux people. In the fall of 1933, with the commencement of the dam project, Fort Peck town site, planned and built by the Army Corps of Engineers to house its employees, began its orderly development.

The construction of the dam spawned shanty boomtowns that were scattered around the work area. These places disappeared almost as quickly as they grew. Some, including New Deal, are now covered by the lake.

Fort Peck Dam is one of the largest earth-filled river impediments in the world. Its original purpose was not only to control floods, but also to create jobs in an economy saddled by depression. At that time, the undertaking was the nation's largest public works project. At its peak in 1936, the building of the dam provided 10,456 jobs. A photograph of the head gates of the dam was featured on the first cover of *Life Magazine*, Nov. 23, 1936.

The Missouri River leaves Fort Peck Lake through the dam's spillway and runs clear again much as it did from its birthplace. In its natural state before the dams, the river was known for its silt and mud. It was at one time estimated that in each million gallons of water, 120 tons of silt were suspended. Steamboats plying the river had to continually clean mud from their boilers.

Within 10 miles of exiting Fort Peck and after regenerating a channel, the Missouri meets the Milk River. The extremely silt-laden waters of the Milk are pushed aside by the stronger flow of the Missouri as it fights to keep the murky color at bay. The intense contrast of the two flows creates a light colored banner along the north bank until finally, the Milk gives up and succumbs to the mightier Missouri.

Meriwether Lewis, May 8, 1805: "*the water of this river posseses a peculiar whiteness, being about the colour of a cup of tea with the admixture of a tabelspoonfull of milk. from the colour of it's water we called it Milk river. we think it possible that this may be the river called by the Minitares* (Hidatsa) *'the river that scolds at all others'* ...." Lewis also noted the Milk River Hills that rise almost 700 feet above the floodplain of the Milk and Missouri. These can be ascended on their south side and reached via Montana Hwy 24 across Fort Peck Dam. From these points, much of the terrain Lewis and Clark described can be viewed, both along the Missouri on the north side of the hills and southwest out over Fort Peck Lake.

When discussing the Missouri, it is important to include the internationally flavored, 538-mile-long Milk River, which pulls its waters from the front range of the Rockies by way of three main tributaries, the North, Middle and South forks tumbling off the Hudson Bay Divide in Glacier National Park. Initially, the Milk is a product of the confluence of the Middle and South forks directly north of Browning, just below Canada. From this point, it slithers northeastward through the middle of Blackfeet Reservation rangeland until it crosses the Canadian line, 47 miles after its start. In Canada, it will pick up its North Fork.

After experiencing 167 Canadian miles, the Milk decides to return stateside just north of the Hi-Line town of Rudyard. Thirty miles later, it enters the long and narrow Fresno Reservoir west of Havre. This basin will control the downriver tempo of the river. After slipping out of its confinement, the Milk River meanders through Havre and follows U.S. Hwy 2 eastward, continually switching from one side of the highway to the other.

Though sluggish and brown-colored, the Milk River provides much needed irrigation on the northern Montana prairie. While the river itself doesn't have the splendor of some its peers, the prairie country it visits is quite beautiful.

Following Havre, the towns of Chinook, Harlem and Dodson get a glimpse of the waterway. Between Harlem and Dodson, on U.S. Hwy 2, the Milk forms the northern boundary of the Fort Belknap

▲ McGarry Bottoms looking towards Dauphin Rapids.

RICK AND SUSIE GRAETZ

◄ Pulling into a Lewis and Clark campsite of May 27, 1805.

RICK AND SUSIE GRAETZ

▲ Bullwhacker Creek area and the Missouri River.
RICK AND SUSIE GRAETZ

▶ Cow Island, historic river crossing and steamboat landing.
RICK AND SUSIE GRAETZ

Indian Reservation, home to the Assiniboine and Gros Ventre nations. Beyond Fort Belknap, the town of Malta embraces the river. At this ranching community, the Milk makes a short run to the north and then begins a southeastward direction, passing Hinsdale and Glasgow on its way to the Missouri.

As the Missouri rolls eastward, the meanders increase as do the sand bars and islands. While the Missouri is still dynamic through its final 185 Montana miles, it doesn't have the strength it had before Fort Peck Dam was completed, and it only drops 220 feet in that last distance. Looking a bit more civilized than the segment between Fort Benton and Fort Peck, it is still, for the most part, void of people.

On May 7, 1804, just southwest of the small community of Frazer, Lewis gave praise. *"The country we passed today ... is one of the most beautiful plains we have yet seen, it rises gradually from the river bottom ... then becoming level as a bowling green ... as far as the eye can reach."*

Poplar, headquarters for the Assiniboine and Sioux tribes, was named for the widespread stands of poplar trees on the riverbanks. Here, the Poplar River comes in from the north and the Redwater River adds a small amount of moisture on the south. The southern boundary of the Fort Peck Indian Reservation is defined by about 130 miles of the Missouri, extending from the mouth of the Milk to the Big Muddy River.

The Corps of Discovery overnighted at present-day Poplar on May 3, 1805, and the captains named the *"Porcupine* (Poplar) *River,"* because of the multitude of needled creatures inhabiting the place. Lewis penned that night, *"the country in this neighborhood of this river, and as far as the eye can reach is level, fertile, open and beatifull beyond description."*

▲ The Missouri near Fred Robinson Bridge.

RICK AND SUSIE GRAETZ

They also christened the present Redwater River, *"2000 mile creek,"* estimating it was 2,000 miles from St. Louis. Many of the places Lewis and Clark designated lost the original names owing to the delay in the publishing of their journals. Others who followed, not knowing the sites already had a label, gave them different monikers.

There are several accounts of how Wolf Point, the next burg on our trip, took its name. The most accepted version was that during a miserable 1860's winter, *"wolfers"* killed several hundred gray wolves that froze before they could be skinned for their pelts. The hunters stacked the carcasses in high piles at their camp along the Missouri and waited for the spring thaw. Indians took over the landing and camp before the skins could be removed; the putrid piles remained. They became a visible and scented landmark, especially to the steamboats coming up river that spring.

Documentation of Wolf Point's exact beginnings is hard to come by. An 1834 map noted an Indian fort at the location. As a settlement, it was probably first established as a trading post for the fur trade. It became a cow town when huge cattle herds, up from Texas and elsewhere, came through on their way to the rich and tall grasses of northern Montana. The place was a genuine frontier outpost and featured a dugout hotel along the river.

In 1914, Wolf Point benefited from a growth spurt brought on by the arrival of farmers when Congress opened up the Fort Peck Reservation to homesteading by non-Indians.

Just above the town of Culbertson, the Milk River slowly works its way south from Canada to join the Missouri. Named for Alexander Culbertson, an early-day fur trapper from the American

▲ Between Cabin and Wagon coulees — Fort Peck Lake.
RICK AND SUSIE GRAETZ

An old homestead stands silent along the Missouri.

RICK AND SUSIE GRAETZ

From the CMR National Wildlife Refuge looking towards the Little Rocky Mountains.

RICK AND SUSIE GRAETZ

From Tripp Divide looking across the Missouri to the UL Bend.

RICK AND SUSIE GRAETZ

Fur Company, the burg got its start about 1888 and is considered to be one of the oldest towns in eastern Montana.

A couple of miles southeast of Culbertson, the Hwy 16 bridge crosses the Missouri. The sweeping river view from here is a favorite of photographers. Beyond the bridge, with 34 miles left before the Missouri prepares to leave Montana and take on the Yellowstone, it rolls through a beautiful mix of bluffs, canyons and badlands. Continually impressed with the pleasant appearance of the landscape, William Clark declared *"the Countrey on both Sides have a butifull appearance."*

The Mandans and Hidatsa had warned of the ferocious white bear the Expedition would encounter. Lewis took this admonition from the natives, who didn't posses guns, lightly, assuming that his superior firepower would more than compensate. On April 29, sometime during midday, before reaching today's Culbertson Bridge, Lewis met his first grizzly. He shot the animal, which then pursued him for almost 80 yards before a second bullet killed it. Lewis, who now gained a new respect for this *"furious and formidable anamal that will frequently pursue the hunter when wounded,"* said, *"these bear being so hard to die reather intimedates us all; I must confess that I do not like the gentelmen and had rather fight two Indians than one bear."*

A few miles before leaving Montana, the Missouri passes Snowden Bridge and the site of the former village of Nohly, where Lewis and Clark and their crew spent their first night in what would become Montana on April 27, 1805. As Lewis began writing in his journals that night, the words he put on paper represent the first written history of Montana.

Sandstone formations near Devils Creek on the CMR National Wildlife Refuge.
RICK AND SUSIE GRAETZ

"This morning I walked through the point formed by the junction of the rivers ... here a beautifull level low plain commences and extends up both rivers for many miles, widening as the rivers recede from each other, and extending back half a mile to a plain about 12 feet higher than itself; ... on the Missouri about 2½ miles from the entrance to the Yellowstone river, and between this high and low plain, a small lake is situated about 200 yards wide extending along the edge of the high plain parallel with the Missouri about one mile." His reference is to Nohly Lake, in close proximity to the town of Fairview.

Once this historic spot is passed, the Missouri appropriates the Yellowstone River just beyond the Montana border with North Dakota. As the river takes leave, it continues to carry the direction and determination it had when it left the three forks. It still has a long way to go before catching the Mississippi, but it has left the finest landscapes of its journey behind in Montana.

▲ Fort Peck Lake at sunrise-low water.

LARRY MAYER

Fort Peck Dam.
CHUCK HANEY

The Milk River before it meets the Missouri.
CHUCK HANEY

▲ Fort Peck Lake has 1,600 miles of shoreline.
RICK AND SUSIE GRAETZ

▶ Missouri River Badlands near Jordan.
RICK AND SUSIE GRAETZ

▲ The Missouri River Breaks near Culbertson.
LARRY MAYER

◀ Confluence of the Yellowstone and Missouri Rivers.
LARRY MAYER

MONTANA'S MUSSELSHELL RIVER

"The trail ran up a creek which kept getting smaller as we went along. Then it went over a low range of hills. When we came to the top of the hill, we could see that we were coming to our promised land at last. As we stood up there, Balboa gazing on the Pacific did not have anything on us. The Musselshell country was a beautiful land. A person could stand in the same place and see buffalo, deer and elk, all at the same time without turning his head." Andrew Garcia from *Tough Trip Through Paradise* — Montana in 1878–1879.

Launched by springs and creeks on the eastern fringe of the Northern Rocky Mountains, the North and South forks of the Musselshell River pour out of the Crazies, Castles and Little Belts, cutting their way through the last ridges and hills of Montana's mountainous province before joining and forming the Musselshell River.

Bonding of the tributaries takes place in a mixture of wetlands and pasture that spreads onto a prairie landscape heading toward the sunrise and the beginnings of Montana east of the mountains. From this simple start, the Musselshell will twist and turn for 364 miles through the heart of Montana, an area geography short on human presence and long on gentle beauty.

The river's past was only yesterday and its annals collect most all the chapters of our state's bygones. It ran the gauntlet from the natives and the first explorers and exploiters to the days of the prospector, the big sheep and cattle empires, the coming of the railroad, and the arrival and demise of the homesteaders.

Its final thrust empties into the Missouri River, in a place that witnessed centuries of passage by the original claimants to the land, the great Indian nations and Montana's initial days of white history. Long before the white invaders came into the Musselshell, the indigenous clans prized the valley as prime hunting territory. No one tribe controlled the Musselshell; instead, it was shared or fought over. The River Crow settled there for a while, but were forced to move south with the formation of the Crow Reservation in 1868.

Indians gave the legendary river its name. As the Hidatsa and Mandan described the landmarks Meriwether Lewis and William Clark should look for on their journey west, they told of the freshwater mussels to be found in a river the explorers would meet after *"the river that scolds all others,"* the Milk River. Clark wrote in his journal, *"The Minetarres (Hidatsa) inform us that this river heads in the 1st of the rocky Mountains & passes through a broken Countrey its head at no great distance from the Yellow Stone River."* How accurately they described the location of the Musselshell! Lewis called it *"Shell river"* or *"Muscle Shell,"* and so penned it on May 21, 1805. The moniker took hold, albeit with a different spelling. Hal Stearns, in his book *The Upper Musselshell Valley of Montana*, states W.W. DeLacy, a mapmaker of note in the 1860s, spelled it *"Musclshell"* and that *"this spelling persisted until November, 1879. From that time on, the river and valley were spelled Musselshell."* Stearns speculates that it was the U.S. Post Office that changed the spelling.

Cattle and sheep were the catalyst to advance settlement of the Musselshell Valley. Ranchers came together to take advantage of free grass amid an unfenced land. An organization of cattlemen called the Musselshell Association gathered all of the herds in the entire 150 miles of the valley. The cowboys

moved the cattle along the range into strategically placed corrals, then eventually brought them together and sorted out the herds by brand. A single roundup could have 60 men and 300 head of horses.

Sheep, especially in the Martinsdale region, were just as important as cows. Imported in 1876, they actually appeared on the range before the bovines. Throughout the time of unfettered land in the Musselshell, the big cattle outfits, in an out-of-character move, shared the range with the huge sheep ranches.

Railroads came next in the line of succession that brought people to the valley. First, there were the smaller lines, the Jawbone and Montana railroads; then the big one, the Milwaukee, with which the history and fortunes of the Musselshell Valley were inextricably linked for more than 70 years.

The Chicago, Milwaukee & St. Paul Railroad Company was already an established Midwest transport business when in 1905, management determined a need to expand westward to Seattle and tweaked its name to Chicago, Milwaukee, St. Paul & Pacific, but in Montana, it remained the "*Milwaukee Railroad.*" Tracks began entering Montana from South Dakota in 1906. One of the main objectives of the route was the agriculturally significant Musselshell Valley which lay between the Great Northern and Northern Pacific realm. The Milwaukee reached the valley in 1908. Rails of the Jawbone Railroad, later the Montana Road, owned by Richard Harlow were already in place along part of the planned way. The Milwaukee first leased, then bought Harlow's right-of-way.

The Milwaukee line ran along the Musselshell River between Melstone and Martinsdale, then climbed through the river's South Fork over Summit and descended to the Smith River Valley.

▲ Lennep in the South Fork of the Musselshell Valley — Crazy Mountains in the distance. RICK AND SUSIE GRAETZ

The valley of the South Fork of the Musselshell just east of Lennep.
RICK AND SUSIE GRAETZ

In building the route, workers moved the river's channel more than 100 times, something that could never be done today.

In 1915, the corporation announced it would electrify its engines between Harlowton and Avery, Idaho. This proved to be an efficient and less expensive way to operate. The engines that pushed the trains uphill traveled backward downhill, using both brakes as generators to recharge electricity used on inclines.

Milwaukee promotion campaigns convinced would-be settlers to move to central Montana. Towns sprang up along some of the sidings and *"sodbusters"* grabbed up bottomland.

A combination of the Homestead Acts, railroad *"hucksterism"* and years of adequate rain brought homesteaders to the Musselshell from 1900 through 1917. A series of droughts commencing in 1917, followed by the Great Depression emptied the land. Faded hopes and dreams became the order of the day throughout the Musselshell Valley. Those able to hang on left relatives who are now the pillars of the communities the river touches.

The Milwaukee's struggles under huge debt and competition from other lines forced it to end its Montana service in 1980.

The present Musselshell country is the epitome of the old and the real Montana. It is free of big towns, sprawl, interstate highways and trinket shops. Uncluttered space dominates. The populace is unobtrusive and of the land; multi-generation ranches and farms are the mainstay. Cattle, sheep, canvas-topped wagons and other signs of agriculture fit in well.

Meagher, Wheatland, Golden Valley, Musselshell, Petroleum and Garfield counties all claim the river. Combined, their population in 1990 was 11,191 and as of the 2000 census, it was 11,502. The towns of Roundup, White Sulphur Springs, Harlowton and Ryegate hold 37 percent of the inhabitants. Roundup, with its 1,931 citizens, is by far the largest hamlet.

Founding tributaries of the river start in high terrain and drop through a mix of forest, meadows and sage-covered hillsides, and then combine in level topography at 4,700 feet. From this modest elevation, the Musselshell loses altitude slowly. Descending at the average rate of about seven feet per mile of riverbed, it finds its way to the Missouri River's channel at 2,160 feet

Embarking on an eastward course, the Musselshell traverses 132 air miles through Montana's heartland before its identity is lost to the Missouri. In doing so, it displays what many folks consider to be the most beautiful drive in the state.

Near Martinsdale, as the valley widens and the main river is sent on its way, the loftiest summits of the Crazy Mountains rise on the south. The clear profile of the eastern extremity of the Little Belt Mountains is to the north. The river takes this view a fair distance, then as the jagged Crazies and the low arc of the Little Belts begin fading in the rearview mirror, the elongated mass of the Big Snowy Mountains rises with a north bearing as an island in central Montana's high plains. Now the Musselshell is on the prairie and as it moves toward the east, these mountains soon begin disappearing below the curvature of the horizon.

The valley deepens near Ryegate and the road climbs a couple of grades, opening up views of the land and the benches above it. This panorama sprawls across a magnificent piece of Montana.

A common thread runs through the makeup of the terrain. Forests of Ponderosa pine and juniper contrast against the cottonwoods of the river bottoms. In some places, the land opens, in others, it

Where you go *"to be seen"* in Martinsdale.

RICK AND SUSIE GRAETZ

▲ The North Fork of the Musselshell River and Bair Reservoir east of White Sulphur Springs.
RICK AND SUSIE GRAETZ

closes in as the canyon deepens; the distant vista hidden by sandstone bluffs and low hills. Relief is kept to a minimum. There is no doubt this is ranch country.

Beyond the town of Roundup, the mountains are out of sight and the country spreads to even larger proportions. Here the earth and sky fuse together without interruption.

Geologically speaking, most of the Musselshell landscape is simple and made of sedimentary rocks. Limestone outcrops in the canyon of the North Fork are followed by shale and sandstone for most of the stream's journey. Near Roundup, the river meets the Fort Union coal formations and as it turns north at Melstone, it is just on the edge of the Williston Basin oil pools.

As the centerpiece of the Upper Musselshell, the Castle Mountains, a massif of 8,000-foot peaks, provide ample water to the tentacles of the river from the north and south and are in essence the Musselshell's primary birthing ground. Their name was attained from ridge top spires, resembling castle turrets, which dominate the visible igneous rocks of the western fringe of the range. Some reach more than 50 feet into the sky. The sedimentary limestone of the eastern rim isn't conducive to creating steeples, but it's the contact zone of the eastside sedimentary and westside igneous rocks that allowed the development of the intense mineralization in this uplift. Old prospector trails crisscrossing the forest canyons and ridgelines are remnants of when the historic Castles boasted the largest silver and lead ore mine in Montana.

In 1885 and 1886, Lafe Hemsly and his three brothers staked mining claims in the area. Two hundred other settlers promptly followed and soon, underground mining for the rich veins of silver and lead commenced and the boomtown of Castle sprang into being. A bank, two hotels, four newspapers, a dance hall, a church, a schoolhouse, a jail and 14 saloons were some of the established structures. Calamity Jane ran one of the restaurants. A stage line provided daily service to White Sulphur Springs, Townsend and Livingston.

Lafe Hemsly's Cumberland Mine was the richest of all. In September, 1891, it was responsible for a $40,000 monthly payroll. The Cumberland was doing so well that a New York capital firm purchased it and about 20 other nearby properties.

By 1891 there were 1,500 to 2,000 people in the area; but almost as hastily as the town grew, it died, never to recover. Folks began leaving the area in droves when the price of bullion drastically dropped in the silver panic of 1893. Now, Castle and its collection of buildings stand silent.

During this time miners felt a railroad from Helena would provide an easier, less expensive way to get their ore to the smelters. The line started on the Missouri River south of Townsend, crossed the mountains at Ringling, climbed to Lennep and on to Castle. By the time the rails reached the disappearing mine camp in 1896, it was far too late. Supposedly the name "*Jawbone*" was given to the railroad because of the persuasive talk of its promoters. Eventually, it continued through the Musselshell Valley to Harlowton and was known as the Montana Railroad, before ownership passed to the Milwaukee.

Lee Rostad, prominent Montana author, who with her husband Phil ranches in the Upper Musselshell near the South Fork's first tide, knows the terrain well. A description, in her words, follows.

"*It's good land ... a valley between the Crazy Mountains to the south and the Castle Mountains to the north. The elevation is over 6,000 in places. The divide at Loweth was the highest point on the railroad east of the Continental Divide.*

"*Indians camped in the valley. Later, the settlers found rock hammers when they plowed an alfalfa field and spotted teepee rings along the higher banks of the stream.*

"*At the western end of the basin, the summit divides the drainages between the South Fork of the Smith River and the South Fork of the Musselshell. The settlement at the top was naturally called Summit, later changed to Loweth. When the railroad was built through, Summit supported a hotel for rail workers and later passengers. Its post office operated from 1915 to 1918. The eventual name alteration was for C.F. Loweth, chief engineer on the Milwaukee Railroad. The Loweth post office was closed in 1924, but the substation for the railroad and a half dozen railroad houses remained until the 1950s. Today, Loweth consists of a brick shell that was once the substation, a Montana Power post, the shipping yards for cattle, some foundations and a couple of apple trees.*

"*A few miles from Loweth, Warm Spring Creek, which rises in the Castles, and the Bozeman Fork Creek, which comes from the Crazies, join to form the South Fork of the Musselshell. Twenty-seven miles from Loweth, the South Fork joins the North Fork at Martinsdale.*"

Lee adds: "*The upper river tributary is predominantly Norwegian and most people are related and that adds to a way of life that is close, but often very structured as the young people work into the fabric of the community. A surprising number return after school or another career.*"

Distinctive for its often-photographed white Lutheran church of 1910 vintage, Lennep sits approximately halfway between Summit and Martinsdale. In 1899, the Montana Railroad gave birth

▲ The Bair Mansion near Martinsdale.
RICK AND SUSIE GRAETZ

▶ Handcrafted woodpeckers are the mascots of the Musselshell Valley.
RICK AND SUSIE GRAETZ

to the town and it continued to serve as a station for the Milwaukee Road. Lennep received its name from a conductor who named it in honor of his hometown, Lennep, Germany. Not much is left of this once thriving place save the church, schoolhouse and a few buildings.

Passing Lennep, the South Fork enters a wider valley and meanders through the sheep grazing grounds of the old Bair family ranch, operating until recently as a museum, before joining the North Fork.

Exploring the North Fork requires a visit to the town of White Sulphur Springs. Positioned west of the divide separating the drainages of the Musselshell and Smith rivers, the town is physically just on the border of the Musselshell country. However, as the seat of Meagher County, which asserts ownership of all of the geography of the river's headwaters, it is entitled to be part of the Musselshell's domain.

For many years, Indians used the area's hot springs. James Brewer, a traveler on the Carroll Trail, noticed them, and in 1866 built a stage stop and developed the springs for travelers. However, it was the successful pursuit of cattle and sheep ranching that grew the town, although the mineral waters were, and still are, a draw.

Verle and Patricia Rademacher, publishers of the *Meagher County News*, have been in White Sulphur Springs for 37 years. Verle feels the community is stable because of agriculture, the Forest Service and recreation opportunities. He also touts the fact that the hydrological divide east of town is the true central Montana watershed as it sends waters in all four compass directions.

The Musselshell's North Fork drifts out of the Little Belts northeast of White Sulphur Springs and just south of Lost Fork Ridge, eventually finding its way south to the Bair Reservoir. It departs that man-made lake in an easterly flow.

West of the reservoir, between mileposts 58 and 59, near the Jamison Trail off the south side of Hwy 12, a couple of prospectors uncovered a copper deposit on July 5, 1866. Staking their claims, they named their camp Copperopolis. The area was mined on and off for several years, but the discovery never lived up to its initial promise. All that is left today is a mine dump.

In the summer of 1867, about 10 miles from Copperopolis, Fort Howie was assembled as a line of defense against the perceived threat of attacks during the so-called "*Indian Wars*" of 1867. Three months after completion, the fort was abandoned. Its location was east of Checkerboard in a hay meadow on the north side of the road at about milepost 69.

The North Fork touches the summer fishing retreat of Checkerboard just down from Bair Reservoir. In 1920, the Sumpter Inn was built here; and then in 1945, the name was changed to Checkerboard after a stream in the area. Fifteen miles east of this place, the North Fork meets its kin from the south and the Musselshell begins its surge.

Martinsdale serves as a human outpost a short distance south of the confluence. The town began in 1876 as Gauglersville when Frank Gaugher built a store along the Carroll Trail. Then Richard Clendennin went into competition against Gaugher, building another store and a hotel in 1877. In 1878, Clendennin was successful in his bid for a postal route and renamed the trading post Martinsdale after Martin Maginnis, a territorial delegate to the U.S. Congress who never lived there. When Richard Harlow's Jawbone Railroad came through in 1899, the town was moved two miles to its present location.

Charlie Bair, one of the most prominent men in the development of agriculture in the Musselshell, began ranching in 1891, and up until 1910 he held a grazing lease in Crow Country near the Yellowstone. Somewhere in between these years, he went to the gold mines of the Yukon and made his fortune promoting a machine that pressurized and heated water, a boon to mining gold in the frozen Klondike. He returned to Montana with plenty of capital.

Bair lost the reservation lease in 1910 and moved all of his operations to Martinsdale. In the '20s and '30s, he proceeded to buy large tracts of land as it became available. He also bought ownership in the Martinsdale Land and Livestock Company and became the majority shareholder. It has been estimated that at one time prior to 1920, he had more than 300,000 head of sheep, one of the largest herds in the world!

Charlie Bair died in 1943 at 85 years old. He had arrived in Montana in 1883, working for the Northern Pacific Railway as a conductor. He left immense wealth and a legacy. His family, especially his daughters, were philanthropic to the hilt. Their home at Martinsdale, then housing an incredible collection of antiques and artifacts, became the Bair Family Museum after the death of Alberta, the last surviving member of the family who died in 1993 at the age of 98.

Martinsdale now serves local ranchers, hunters and anglers. Some of the old buildings including the depot, still remain. A bank stands out as a remnant of the homestead days. The Crazy Mountain Inn, built in 1901, has been renovated and does a lively business. Sheep once found in large numbers still graze the fields and hills surrounding the town.

Gordon Butte, just on the west edge of Martinsdale, is a prominent Musselshell landmark and perhaps the final outlier of the Northern Rockies along the river. Geologists Dave Alt and Don Hyndman call it *"an outpost of the Crazy Mountains resembling a giant hockey puck."* More than a mile in diameter and about 700 feet high, this *"laccolith"* is an almost perfectly circular intrusion of molten rock, created when a blister of magma was injected into the area's sedimentary rocks.

Two Dot, named for early-day cattleman *"Two Dot"* Wilson, touches the Musselshell River 17 miles below Martinsdale. Wilson's brand consisted of two dots, with one on the shoulder of the animal and another on the thigh, thus making it hard for rustlers to change the mark.

Roberta Cheney, in her book Names on the Face of Montana, tells an interesting story about Wilson. *"'Two Dot' was never one for dressing up, and at one time in Chicago after he had gone there with a load of cattle, he was arrested for vagrancy because he was so dirty and unkempt. He asked the policemen to go to the bank with him. When it was verified that Wilson had just deposited more than $10,000, the policemen let him go. The incident had begun as a practical joke. Two of the cowhands Wilson had brought to Chicago with him decided to play a trick on the boss and pointed him out to the police as vagrant. 'Two Dot' found out about it and went the cowboys one better. He took the next train home and left them in Chicago without any money or return ticket."*

In 1900, the Montana Railroad reached Two Dot facilitating the town's growth. As with every other Musselshell Valley town, the homestead years swelled the population and fostered the expansion of businesses. The 1910s were heady days — until the drought changed everything.

Nineteen miles from Two Dot, Harlowton, county seat of Wheatland County, guards the river. *"Harlo,"* as it is commonly called, is a crossroads of travel from the Yellowstone River country, the Musselshell Valley and the Judith Basin. Richard Harlow, developer of the Jawbone and the Montana Railroad, laid his tracks toward the small settlement of Merino. As an act of gratitude, the town folks changed the name to Harlowton. When the Milwaukee bought out the Montana Road, Harlowton

From Two Dot, looking west up the Musselshell Valley.

RICK AND SUSIE GRAETZ

A tribute to the Milwaukee Railroad era at Harlowton.

RICK AND SUSIE GRAETZ

▲ The lonely remains of Barber in the Musselshell Valley.
RICK AND SUSIE GRAETZ

▶ The Musselshell River near Ryegate
RICK AND SUSIE GRAETZ

served as the division switching point. Trains headed east had steam locomotives put in place of their electric engines, and westbound trains dropped their steamers in exchange for electric engines.

Harlowton's main street is typical of most small Montana towns, neat and orderly, but with vacant buildings. Local quarries provided sandstone for storefronts constructed by immigrant stonemasons who had developed their trade in Europe. As a result, part of the downtown is preserved as an historic district.

Agriculture is now the town's bread and butter. Gerald Miller, publisher and editor of The Times-Clarion, Harlowton's newspaper, says that when the Milwaukee pulled out in 1980, there were 125 jobs lost. Many of the workers managed to stay in the area and Miller considers that the town's economy should remain firm. The potential for wind-generated electrical power in the Judith Gap area is real and he would like to see restoration of the historic Graves Hotel finished as an attraction to more visitors. The grand old edifice was named for A.C. Graves, an early 1900s Harlowton promoter.

The Times-Clarion was the longtime domain of legendary Montana newspaperman and historian Hal Stearns, who wrote extensively on the Upper Musselshell. Stearns, who died in 2004, owned the newspaper from 1941 until 1973. The current publisher began working for Stearns in 1948, and then bought the weekly in 1973.

Judith Gap, a broad wind-swept divide between the Big Snowy and Little Belt mountains, north of the Musselshell, carries Hwy 191 to the river valley at Harlowton. Indians following the bison used the path over this prairie pass for centuries. In the 1870s, stage and freight lines traversed the old Carroll Trail that crossed through the Gap. Later, the Great Northern and Milwaukee railroads laid track over it.

East of Harlowton, and beyond where the road over the Judith Gap meets the Musselshell, the river edges closer to the roadway. The wide-open valley begins narrowing somewhat, the river canyon deepens and heavy cottonwood growth begins to show. Approaching Ryegate, the sandstone rimrocks that the river is known for become more plentiful.

Shawmut, about 17 miles from Harlowton, is a small outpost north of the river with a collection of buildings from the early part of the 1900s. Named after a local rancher, it is sheep country.

Just beyond Shawmut, and a bit south of the highway, sits the former town site of Barber. Platted in 1910 by Henry Bartz, today, only a couple of old buildings and a church are left. But in 1920, there was a bank, a hotel, a general store, an implement store, a post office and a church. Originally, Barber was named Shawmut. When the railroad needed more land and ranchers refused to sell, the train depot was literally picked up and moved by rail eight miles to the west and the "*new*" Shawmut came into being. Roberta Cheney mentions in , that someone from the original Shawmut "*quipped that they had been given a clean shave and should change the name to Barber — and so they did.*"

As the homesteaders left Barber, the general store and post office managed to stay open until the late '50s. By the end of the 1970s, only the church was still viable, and it remains so to this day.

Fifteen miles east of Shawmut and on the north side of the river, Ryegate, the seat of Golden Valley County, is propped up against a three-mile-long sandstone bluff. A railroad official noticed fields of rye on the then Sims-Garfield Ranch, and named the town after the crop. Ryegate holds the distinction of being home to Montana's first woman sheriff, Ruth Garfield. In 1920, after her husband was killed, she was appointed to finish the remaining two years of his term. As county seat, Ryegate

A bird's eye view of the Musselshell River Valley.

LARRY MAYER

holds local government jobs that add some permanence lacking in other nearby towns.

Sixteen miles below Ryegate, Lavina is on the north bank of the Musselshell at the junction of Montana Hwy 3 and U.S. Hwy 12. Highway 3 serves as Lavina's main street and leads south to Billings. For a time, the place was called *"White City"* because the residents had a penchant for painting most of the structures there white.

Records show two different versions of how it became Lavina. One claims it was named for the daughter of the housekeeper of an early settler named Vance. Other historical notes say it was named for the girlfriend of Walter Burke, who was hired in 1882 by frontier merchant Thomas Power of Fort Benton, to establish a stage stop on the 220-mile road between Fort Benton and Billings.

Two prominent vintage structures, the Adams Hotel and Slayton Mercantile, are reminders of a different era in Lavina. Now closed, The Adams served travelers on the trail for many years. The Mercantile is the town's social center. Lavina's post office was opened in 1883.

Heading east of Lavina, the river is out of sight of Hwy 12 for about 10 or 12 miles. It is 23 miles from Lavina to Roundup where Hwy 87 wanders up from Billings to the south. Along the way, the Bull Mountains, a coal bearing sedimentary uplift, come into view on the southeast. Coal found here was used to fuel the steam engines of the Milwaukee Railroad.

The highest points of this 50-mile-long range of low mountains are just over 4,000 feet. Their sandstone benches separate the Missouri and the Yellowstone river basins and provide water to the Musselshell. In recent years, fires have ravaged the Bulls, once heavily timbered.

"Capital of the Bulls," Roundup is the largest town on the Musselshell. Nearly 2,000 folks call it home. In 1882, just beneath the sandstone rimrocks, a couple built a saloon and store near where Half Breed Creek and the Musselshell meet. The post office opened in 1883.

The town became known for coal and the Milwaukee Railroad, but the moniker comes from the 1880 days of the open range. A short distance west of where the town now lies, cowboys met from throughout the Musselshell to participate in their annual roundup.

When the Milwaukee Railroad made it here in 1907, the town's demeanor changed dramatically and growth took off. The company established the Republic Coal Company when it laid its tracks into Roundup. In essence it became a company town, although the actual coal mining camp of Klein was located two miles to the south. The unfenced, free grass times were long gone, ended by an influx of homesteaders. Although ranching persisted, the cowboy posture was lost for sometime to come.

A Milwaukee Railroad historian claimed, *"The Milwaukee Road became Roundup's modern founder, employer and provider."* By 1913, 3,000 people called the area home, many of them from across the Atlantic.

Roundup's Musselshell Museum's historical records estimated at one time 600 miners dug enough coal to fill a railcar every 12 minutes. One vertical shaft in an area mine was dug 287 feet into the ground.

Today, coal mining, the Milwaukee Railroad and the homesteaders have departed, but a stable community lingers on.

Twenty-three miles east of Roundup, just south of Hwy 12 on the southern side of the river, is the village of Musselshell. Now a mere shadow of its former self, it at one time was called *"The Crossing"* and was the only spot between Fort Maginiss near Lewistown and Fort Custer on the Yellowstone

River to traverse the Musselshell.

By the 1870s, many large cattle companies drove their herds up from Texas to winter on the rich grasses in the valleys of central Montana. The crossing at Musselshell was considered the last stop on the Texas Trail. From here, the livestock spread out to the north to forage the open range.

In 1880, Larry Reed and his Crow wife built a cabin and a store on the south bank near the original ford called *"Lower Crossing,"* giving birth to what would become Musselshell. For a brief period the place was called *"Reed's Crossing."* A post office opened in 1883, presumably under the name Musselshell. As the town grew, newspaper accounts touted it as the *"Metropolis of the Valley"* and for a time it was the largest settlement along the river.

Adair Rademacher, a member of the local water board, explained that today there are only 40 water users, but at one time there were five or six saloons, two banks and two dry goods stores. She points out that the Handel brothers were responsible for the fact that the town didn't get even bigger. It seems the Milwaukee Railroad was approaching the area and had asked the men to donate some of their land for a right of way. They refused, and as a result, the train roundhouse for the railroad was established farther east at Melstone.

Mrs. Rademacher said it was coal and the railroad that attracted people to the town, especially Eastern Europeans. Not only did they know how to mine coal, but they also *"were the only ones willing to work hard enough to lay railroad track in the hot weather experienced on the prairie of central Montana."* Most of the miners worked in the Star Mine, a Bair family holding, northeast of town.

▲ Sandstone cliffs and ranch land are plentiful along the Musselshell.
RICK AND SUSIE GRAETZ

The Star operated pumps night and day as some of its tunnels ran under the Musselshell River.

A sturdy red brick building, still enduring in Musselshell, was once the Hotel Stockwell. Built by Mrs. Stockwell, whose two daughters married the Handel brothers.

The yellow firebrick school building, no longer needed as schoolhouse, was given to the town to be used as a community center on July 1, 2003.

Melstone, 14 miles farther downriver, was named for Melvin Stone, an Associated Press reporter who was aboard a train with the Milwaukee's president when the rails first achieved this area. The town, a beneficiary of the Handel brothers' refusal to donate land, was also more populated than Musselshell during the homestead era and height of the Milwaukee Railroad period. Kim Walker, present-day City Clerk and Treasurer, said there are approximately 129 individuals living in Melstone as of 2003, and that in 1990 the population was rated at 139.

As to the Melstone area, Mrs. Walker states, *"it grows on you and you learn to love it."*

Drought of the past several years has hurt this town that now relies on ranching, although cattle herds are building back. The number of ranches, all multi-generational operations, are staying about the same; in some cases the children are returning to take over management.

Dorothy Minnie was born on a homestead 14 miles from Melstone and lived in the area for 83 years. Mrs. Minnie said that when she was younger, the *"homesteaders didn't travel much ... transportation wasn't available in the area and everyone helped each other out."* Now, she said, *"people go to Billings, 60 miles away, for lunch."* She reminisced that *"as kids they didn't go to town very often and Melstone was quite big."* There were many businesses including banks, at least four grocery stores and three hotels. Once, she and her sister were sent into Melstone to get bread and, Mrs. Minnie said, *"We got lost getting the bread in the downtown area."*

Two miles east of Melstone, at the *"Big Bend of the Musselshell,"* the river makes an abrupt turn to the north and enters landscape considerably drier than the river's course up until this point. Badlands show and the rises are mostly buttes and rock outcroppings. The viewshed is extensive as the river leads into a part of Montana often called *"the Big Open"* and *"the Big Dry."* The Musselshell seems to get lost on this part of the vast prairie as it cuts a canyon through the sandstone. The only giveaways of its presence are glimpses of ribbons of cottonwoods.

According to Dorothy Minnie, this section in the earlier days was sheep, cattle, and homestead country, but she remembers it was always more arid to the north of Melstone.

As well as changing directions, the river leaves Hwy 12 off to the east. County Road 500, mostly gravel for 34 miles to Hwy 200, now follows the stream from a distance. By late summer, this 130-mile stretch to the end of the Musselshell is nearly dewatered. Heat, lack of rain and upstream irrigation add up to a meager substance, if any, to fill the channel. White alkaline deposits often take the place of liquid flow.

Mosby, at the Hwy 200 crossing of the Musselshell, today retains only an abandoned house. In 1891, William and Mary Mosby situated their post office to the east side of the Musselshell crossing and established a ferry. In 1904, they moved farther downriver to the present site and kept a ferry going until a wooden bridge was built in 1918. Since the post office was in their home, it became a center for ranch families as they came to collect their mail.

Mrs. Mosby once wrote a piece for the *Winnett Times*. Speaking of the Musselshell and the Mosby

▲ Many consider the Musselshell to be one of the most beautiful drives in the state.
RICK AND SUSIE GRAETZ

◀ In the Musselshell Valley.
RICK AND SUSIE GRAETZ

Near Rygate.

RICK AND SUSIE GRAETZ

area she noted: *"... it is wild, rugged, spectacularly scenic, lonesome and harsh, but it's good country — very good country. Spring ice jams on the Musselshell turn loose raging floods that cover bottom lands, and tear down fences and strew dead trees and other debris."* The Lewistown News Argus paraphrased the thoughts of homesteaders from the same place: *"We are 80 miles from a doctor and the dirt trails can be knee-deep in mud or belly-deep in snow before the paved highway is reached that will take people to Lewistown, Winnett or Jordan."*

From Mosby, the Musselshell makes its final 74-mile run through a landscape not very often seen. Halfway from its terminus, it enters the crown jewel of our nation's wildlife refuge system, the 1.1-million-acre Charles M. Russell National Wildlife Refuge. The canyon again narrows as the Missouri River Breaks begin.

Where the magical river ends and Fort Peck Lake and the Missouri River start is somewhat nebulous, especially from the air. The Musselshell is silting-in its channel and the lake segment of the Missouri in the area of U.L. Bend. Before Fort Peck Dam's 1940 completion, the free flowing Missouri carried valuable silt from the Musselshell downriver to create new beds for cottonwood seedlings and build islands beneficial to wildlife.

Very quiet now, the Musselshell's terminus was once a place of significance in the time of cattle barons and earlier. Here, vast herds of bison crossed the Missouri on their annual migrations. As a major fording point for the Indians of eastern Montana, battles and skirmishes with the white man and among themselves over hunting rights and other hostilities often occurred there. A succession of fur trading posts, wood yards, military camps, ranches and homesteads at one time or another occupied the area.

The confluence was also a gathering place for horse rustlers and other outlaws. Horse-stealing rings tormented ranchers in the Missouri Breaks in the late 1800s. Raiding ranches in Montana, Wyoming, and the Dakotas, bandits drove the livestock to remote areas of the Breaks in and around the Musselshell, *"worked the brands,"* and then drove them to Canada for sale, repeating the process with stolen Canadian livestock. On the return trip, the outlaws were always on the lookout for the law and vigilantes.

One of the most famous incidents of *"vigilante justice"* occurred in 1884. Granville Stuart, operator of the DHS ranch, led a group of local stockmen to the Musselshell to clean out a large horse-thieving ring. Two outlaws were hanged there and two more suffered the same fate at Rocky Point, upriver on the Missouri. A few days later, these stockmen, who later became known as *"Stuart's Stranglers,"* apprehended more horse thieves at an abandoned wood yard at Bates Point, 15 miles below the mouth of the Musselshell. Five outlaws were killed in the ensuing gun battle. Seven managed to escape, but five of them were later captured by soldiers in eastern Montana and returned to the vigilantes. They were hanged from cottonwoods that grew in the broad flat bottoms of the Musselshell.

The area surrounding the joining of the Missouri and Musselshell may have been the epitome of the old and wild West. Much has been written about it. In 1885, Peter Koch remembered some of the life he had spent at *"Muscleshell"* in 1869 and 1870. *"From Fort Benton to the Yellowstone the country along both sides of the Missouri was as wild as when Lewis and Clark first stemmed its turbid current. It is true that a few trading posts were planted along its banks, that a number of steamboats yearly made their difficult way between and over its sand-bars to Fort Benton or Cow*

▲ East of Roundup
RICK AND SUSIE GRAETZ

◄ Rich grasses brought sheep and cattle to the area in the late 1870s.
RICK AND SUSIE GRAETZ

▲ The town of Lavina sits just off of the Musselshell.
LARRY MAYER

▶ Roundup has the highest population of all the Musselshell towns.
LARRY MAYER

Island, that at rare intervals a clearing had been made around a wood-yard in one of the densely wooded points. But the steamboat passed, and when the sound of its whistle was beyond hearing no sign of its passage was left ... The trading post did not become the nucleus of a village or a center for spreading civilization. It was simply a place to accumulate robes, skins and furs.

"The center of this life on the upper part of the river was the trading post at Muscleshell. To those who landed there early in June 1869, the place presented a characteristic sight. It enjoyed at that time its greatest prosperity and formed quite a little village ... the settlement was ambitious and aspired to become a city. But all those ambitions were destined to disappointment. No military post was established (only camps). The Indian trade declined. With the completion of the Union Pacific Railroad the river route lost importance for a time, and when it was revived not Muscleshell but Carroll was selected as the shipping point. When I left the place the Missouri had already undermined some of the houses, and to-day not a vestige is left to show where the settlement once stood."

Sadly, the Musselshell ends unceremoniously in a sluggish flow; silting is not a pretty way to go out. And in terms of legend and notoriety, the Big Missouri that receives its meager contribution, has a far greater and widespread reputation. At this point then, the Musselshell accepts its status. But to the folks upriver, and to those who know and appreciate Montana's blend of a diverse landscape and history, the Musselshell River is every bit a grand river and a fine asset to the Missouri and Big Sky Country.

▲ The Musselshell Valley north of Melstone.
RICK AND SUSIE GRAETZ

▲ North of Melstone and beyond the big bend where the Musselshell turns north.
RICK AND SUSIE GRAETZ

▶ The confluence of the Missouri and Musselshell rivers at the UL Bend.
LARRY MAYER

MONTANA'S MISSOURI & MUSSELSHELL RIVERS